MR. MANNERS:

Proper Etiquette for the Modern Degenerate

By: Aaron Berg

Paperback Edition

Aaronberg.Com

Artwork by Ricky Letovsky and Jamie Mathieson

nachonightstudios.com

Ash,

May you learn everything you need to know about misogyny +laughter in these pages.

Mr. Manners

Table of Contents

Introduction

What do I know about etiquette? I wasn't raised Baptist or raped as a child, so I'm not over the top with my shit. But I am a nice guy. As asshole-ish as I may seem, I truly go out of my way to be helpful and be aware of others around me. All of the acts that I wrote about in this book are very self-indulgent forms of filth, however they involve other people. Call me the last of the renaissance men, but I still believe that other people matter.

Whether you're yelling the N-word loudly with colleagues, getting blown in a cab by a theatre school princess, doing coke with future hosts of Saturday Night Live, trying to get your penis inside of a handicapped woman or getting your ass kicked outside of a bar; you need to realize that all of these actions involve other people.

I find that people in North America have become incredibly selfish and it's nice to realize once in a while that even though we are pieces of ambitious, self-centered white trash that need these dirty thrills in life, our actions involve other people.

So I wrote an etiquette book for people that traditionally don't use etiquette and for situations that don't traditionally involve etiquette. This will ensure that your colleagues understand why you need to use the N-word to prove that equality exists, that the cabbie driving you while you get blown doesn't get more upset than he has to, that movies stars won't sue you after you do cocaine in Winnipeg with them, that the handicapped woman you're trying to fuck understands that it's because you're non-judgmental and not a tard-rapist, and finally that after you get your ass rightfully kicked that you don't cry like a dirty bitch.

On top of this is another fifty or so incidents that require proper etiquette. Manners need to be present in being a degenerate, otherwise we are nothing more than savages. Read this. Let me know if you have more questions and I will be a martyr and live my life in a way unfit for most so that you may reap the benefits of my experience.

Email me any questions about your white trash lives and I will respond in one way or another…. mrmannersbook@gmail.com Also, thanks for learning to read, you quintessential hillbilly!

Many thanks to the women who so selflessly and unknowingly volunteered to be a part of this book. I never knew at the time of our trysts that I was going to write a book. At least I didn't mention names. Big thanks to the Yuk Yuk's family in Canada. Sincere thanks to Mark Breslin who is always a source of guidance and a gateway to the world of comedy. He has always taught me to avoid being normal, for that I think he should be American. The Cringe Humor family and all the great people that work at The Stand NYC. Since moving to NYC, you've really made me feel at home and I appreciate that. Thanks to Danny and Ricky for helping put this together. Finally, thanks to all of my hilarious friends in New York…there are far too many to list but there are people that are so funny in this city they make me laugh via text.

Proper etiquette for realizing that you are, in fact, a modern degenerate

To be a modern-day degenerate male, one must possess several qualities and not merely just dabble in debauchery. A true degenerate does not necessarily need to begin blossoming in the early stages of life, but it helps. Perhaps when you were 10 years old, you found porno magazines under the train tracks, and that "find" made you curious about the opposite sex. It may have given you an inkling that sex was to be a major factor in your existence.

You may have started to plan for puberty long before it ever happened. You may have repeatedly checked your genitals and waited for the day when they would evolve into the man-like tools that could be used for intercourse. You probably attempted to figure out the opposite sex and studied what made them tick. Maybe at 12 years of age you knew girls liked bad boys and you were already smoking cigarettes, even though it was hard to buy them at that age; you would smoke butts you found in parks and public ashtrays just to plant future "possible pussy" seeds.

You may have had your first sexual experience with other neighborhood guys as you all beat off in a garage and compared pubic hair counts. This weirdness may have set you up for years to come. Then you cherished fingering your first girl. You had no idea what you were doing, so you would finger quickly like the porno films you had studied, thanks to being an 80's porno connoisseur. You delighted in the armpit-like scent that lingered on your index finger for days. You remember your first blowjob from a girl who had braces, and it was in an orange tube slide in a park. SHE WAS A SLUT! She had bragged about her oral capabilities at 16 years of age and you were only too glad to test the truth of her claims. The braces didn't tear up your dick. That was a myth that you had proved false. By the age of 15, you were already a sexual trailblazer.

You would then go on to get more blowjobs and compare them to that first blowjob; many of the early blowjobs could not match up to that first hummer, even though they were braces-free. You probably started trying to drink alcohol at an early age because you knew that it increased your chances of getting sex. You probably didn't like the taste of beer initially. You may have even poured out beer to give the impression that you drank it quickly when people weren't looking so that you could seem like an alcoholic; this made you look cooler than you were. You obviously always hung out with older, more mature people - otherwise, how could you get the beer when you were 16?

These older people helped give you an outsider's perspective, which made you hipper than the people your own age. This allowed you to live off the mainstream grid. You probably started to experiment with drugs, gangs, low-income housing. You acquired a taste for the underbelly of society. You would smoke hash and weed; you looked at people with cool graffiti on their backpacks and wondered who "The Smiths" and "Toad the Wet Sprocket" were. You probably showed up at your parent's house well after curfew several times. You were probably in and out of high schools. You probably got kicked out of your parents' house and stayed in the projects with friends of varying cultural and racial backgrounds.

You may have picked up the ability to speak Jamaican patois by the time you were 17. You may have studied one of the martial arts and then stopped doing it as pussy became more plentiful. But that fighter is still inside of you and willing to come out whenever you need it. You may have gotten arrested for some young offender-type crimes which landed you in jail for a night or two, and then your parents reluctantly bailed you out. This may have actually brought you closer to your parents. You were then shipped off to some school that was supposed to better you. You were not allowed to smoke or drink. You found ways to smoke and drink.

You learned that it's easy to bang private school chicks in the woods, and you learned that ugly girls with good bodies can fuck really well because they have something to prove. You then got an education that was centered on left-wing thought. You learned how to write and to express ideas and the fact that if everybody likes what you're doing, you're doing something wrong. You then obtained some kind of post-secondary education, after which you worked shady bar jobs. You banged more college pussy than a low-grade Hollywood producer.

You got your first, second, and third STDs. You learned that Q-tips go places other than ears and how small your penis can get in a doctor's office. You graduated. You were in and out of jobs, entrepreneurial efforts, passion projects, relationships, apartments, properties you purchased, but you always managed to keep sex at the forefront of your mind. You were a renaissance man; you found the easiest way to do the hardest thing in life, which is to follow your dreams.

Through it all, you were able to drink, smoke, stay up late, and barely avoid mainstream day jobs and homelessness. You have had financial issues constantly, but you always find a way to live. And I don't mean "barely live," like a student on ramen noodles. You found a way to have the best things in life. You have driven sports cars and SUVs. You have partied with famous people and simultaneously shunned fame. You have dined on US Grade AAA beef with movie stars and done GHB with call girls. You may have never been to Vegas because you are too Vegas for Vegas. You don't need to take a plane ride to the desert to know how cool you are.

You have had sex at the top of the CN tower, you have tit-fucked a handicapped girl (consensually) and you have slept with every type of woman. You have had intercourse in all holes and then sat with a girl as she cried after she begged to try anal lovemaking. You then got turned off of anal, because what's the point? If she's gonna cry, you could have just argued. Every morning when you wake up, you may not be excited by what yesterday gave you, but you have hope for the new day.

You live every day like it's your last. And yes, you've made some mistakes, and yes, you've got some problems, and yes, you battle addiction, but goddammit, you wouldn't have it any other way. You are a modern degenerate! Congratulations.

*** You needn't have all of these qualities to be a modern degenerate. One of the aforementioned qualities may be enough to qualify you.

Proper etiquette for dealing with a pregnancy scare

"If the young knew and the old had more goo." There is a saying that kind of goes like that, but it refers more to achieving life's goals and overcoming the hardships of humanity. But in this case the quote refers to bearing children. Not sure if you've looked around your world recently, but for most white people it's hard as four-day-old rabbit shit to have kids. They have to try and try and then look into different adoption services. So here are these exhausted, well-off white couples that could very easily provide for several children and something chooses to smite them. Then they have to run around all willy-nilly looking at various adoption options. Usually the available babies are from overseas.

So instead of having a baby as a result of your combined semen/egg, you need to choose between a Ugandan, a Russian, or some off-the grid, "small village" type of Asian baby. Now we all know that we live in a post-racist world and that you want to say that you are going to love this child just as if it were your own: BUT COME ON!!! We know that something you made is better than something that was shipped to you, although maybe not better at math (if it's an off-the-grid "small village" Asian) or stripping (the Russian) or hunting down gazelles (obviously, the Ugandan).

So why is it so hard for white people to have kids? Why must they fuck endlessly to make one child, when we as teenagers were popping semen bullets off left, right, and center and making babies that we were getting aborted? I think that we just answered a question with a question.

White people are having trouble making babies because of our history of promiscuity. We have had so many abortions and passed so many diseases back and forth that our bodies are incapable of making children. In contrast, other races, which multiply much more rapidly (Ugandans, Russians, off-the-grid "small village" Asians . . . we may also include Puerto Ricans and then allow our kaleidoscope to get more colorful) may have been promiscuous but they never troubled themselves with wasted loads of baby batter being donated to "safe sex" and they never had abortions that scraped the fuck out of the inside of a uterus, rendering it almost as useless as a vehicle torn apart post-accident by the jaws of life.

All of this being said, when we were younger, we had hopes and dreams and didn't want children to get in the way of those hopes and dreams; now that we're older, we've either accomplished those hopes and dreams or realized that our ambition was all for naught and that there is no God and no redemption. Either way, once we hit 40, we want kids. But it's not always like that. In your 20's and 30's, you get a little careless with your dick. It's a powerful weapon and you don't always know how to wield it. You are like a racist man in Florida with a gun and a "Stand your ground" law. You have rights, but you need to know your rights.

Now let's get to this pregnancy scare. First, go have unprotected sex with a woman. It feels way better than protected sex and you will both like it better. Initially, you may start off wearing a condom, but you will notice that it makes your dick floppy. Take the dome off. Go with just the tip for a bit and then trick her and insert all the way. She is probably in heaven now, so you think that she is okay with all of this. Her moans and other signals of pleasure have you thinking that you are a golden god. Now you're thinking, "Should I come inside of her?"

Just as you are about to come in her, you will think better of it and pull out and come all over her belly.

You never talked about whether or not she was on the pill. She may be, she may not be, but either way, you pulled out so you're good, right??? WRONG! You forgot about the pre-come. It's too late now. Good news: if you don't like this woman, you have at least a few weeks before she finds out that she is pregnant. If you have a limited online presence and minimal possessions, you can pack up and leave the country.

Drive to Mexico and tell the border patrol that you are going down for a bachelor party in Cozumel. Then never come back and never answer your phone. Your phone also may not work in Mexico, depending on who your mobile carrier is, how often you pay your bill, and how exorbitant your roaming charges are. By the time she finds out that your drippy pre-come knocked her up, you'll be drunk and balls deep inside of a donkey (if that's your thing).

Now, rewind. If you at all care about this woman, you may have to stick around. First of all, you'll probably want to have more sex with her, because nobody else gives up the unprotected slop box to you. Have sex a few more times that first night: she's already pregnant, she can't get pregnant twice (not a medical fact). Hang out with her and get friendly.

Now in about 3 or 4 weeks, you'll think, "This sex is great!" This chick never messes up the sheets because she is never on her period." SON OF A BITCH!!! Pregnant!!!! Now you have a few options. She will tell you that she missed her period and that she might be pregnant. She is either pregnant, or you gave her HPV. Either way, nobody wins.

Option 1: If you are a Latin man, you will keep the baby. You may be too young and too uneducated to have a kid, but your God, "Jesus - God of the Latinos" believes that this baby will make you work harder to provide for it. The Latin God is wrong. Your child will be cute as a kid but then will grow up to be extremely short and in a gang or a remake of a break-dancing movie.

Option 2: If you are a black man, put this woman in touch with your other baby mommas. Now they will all complain about you and smoke Newports while you are away on your rap tours preaching hate about homosexuals.

Option 3: If you are white and want to keep the baby, you are stupid. It is too early in your life to crush your dreams.

Option 4: Convince her to get rid of the devil seed that you two have created in this dirty little lab she calls her vagina. This has to be done smoothly. YOU CAN NOT FREAK OUT! She is already freaking out. Be compassionate and keep the endgame in mind. Listen to every option she presents. She may say things like, "I wasn't ready for this. I know we weren't planning it, but maybe this is the time."

Tell her that you love her and will support her every decision, but that this is a decision that affects both of your lives. One day you want to have a child with her, but that time is not now. She will usually get on board with this type of logic. Continue to explain that you want the both of you to be settled into your careers and happy so that you can give your children the best life possible. Also, you never want her to feel limited in life because of a child that you were half responsible for.

Continue this logic for a week or so. Be her rock. You cannot get overly emotional at all. We know that you don't want to have the kid, she knows you don't want to have the kid, but she also thinks that it's for unselfish reasons; if you get emotional you may look too selfish. She may be religious and think that God does not want the child killed. In this case, you're fucked. There is no arguing with a political stance that is still a major dilemma even in free countries. Why would you put your dick in this Bible-thumper? YOU SHOULD HAVE DRIVEN TO MEXICO WHEN YOU HAD THE CHANCE!

But if she is not a born-again bumpkin, you have probably convinced her that your lives will be better spent with just the two of you for a while longer. Go and be supportive as she champions the pro-choice movement. You have chosen a strong woman who believes in the ability and power of her own body. Walk past the picketers and the striking Christ-mongers, and know that your life partner is by your side and is a strong woman.

Once she has physically and mentally recovered from the invasive procedure (metallic rape) and you have showered her with gifts and affection . . . time to move on. Whew, you dodged a bullet there. Be nice. She was. Take your time in the breakup and handle this as "one of the exes that you may have actually cared for" in the future. Well done, childless gentleman!

Proper etiquette for dating an actress

Many of us have dreamed of that moment when we get to court a stunning, talented, Oscar winner who can both cry and laugh on cue. We envision dating this goddess with all of her eccentricities and her African foster children and her photo shoots. But that, my friends, is a movie star, and it will not happen for any of us. So allow me to be clear. I'm talking about an actress. These women fall into two categories:

(1) a working actress or

(2) a bartender/waitress who dreams of being an actress.

For all intents and purposes, they are very similar - both are dramatic, insane, sexual, and full of daddy issues. The key difference between the two is the hours. Working actresses get up at 4 a.m., whereas waitresses go to sleep at 4 a.m. So let's focus on a working actress for this lesson.

Find yourself a younger woman. Nobody likes an older actress, especially the industry. Get someone far younger than you but ensure that she is legal. Make sure that she is at least 18 and do not meet her online. To her at this point, life is but a dream, and you are her dream man. She does not know where this is going. Meet her somewhere for a drink. Actresses love to drink until they make some major life mistakes. But she is young and still considers her mistakes to be learning experiences.

Oh yes, her youthful well overflows with optimism. Don't let it bring you down. Drink and bang a lot. You will not need condoms because actresses are risk takers. Improvisers, in particular, will say "Yes and" to everything. Meet her friends. They will think that they are better than you because they have "starred" in commercials, but at the end of the day they are merely pawns in the game of mass-media mediocrity, just low-end beer spokespeople.

Pretend you like her male friends with their white teeth and their gelled hair. Pretend that you like her female friends with their back stabbing and their large tits. Go to parties and drink with them. Flirt with her friends, male and female; after all, these are actors, and even if they are straight, they're at least half gay. You will go home with your actress lover many nights and have sex thinking about her friends. You're close enough you can move in together now. This will kill all the spontaneity.

She will act out on her thoughts about you being a womanizer, but you can merely tell her she is mistaken and it's all in her head. Doing this makes women crazier than they are naturally. Which is what you want, because what's the point of dating a somewhat insane actress? You want your girl mental patient, bat-shit crazy. This will spice things up for a bit, but then you will start smoking weed to avoid dealing with her.

At this point, she will go out and live her life, because that's what actresses do. NO LABELS! She may cheat on you. You will be high enough to believe that whenever she is out, she is in fact cheating on you. This actress is a whore-witch!   She takes her insecurities and places them onto you. Break up with her. It will be messy. Ten years later, she will be a big starlet. You will have grown enough to almost admit when you're wrong.   Invite her to a documentary about you. (If you are not in a documentary, well, cameras are cheap enough these days, and, with the help of a Kickstarter campaign, you should be up and running in a few months).

Look back fondly upon your times together as you drink at the after-party.   Don't sleep together, however, because you are a gentleman. Just know that you will always have a place to stay in Hollywood. And since she'll be working on set all the time, you'll have her place to bang new insane women in.

Well played, vindictive gentleman.

Proper etiquette for hooking up with a handicapped woman

Many of us have had the opportunity to sleep with women who have the gift of being insane. This can stem from past emotional baggage, daddy issues, or mere chemical imbalances and bipolarity. However, stepping into the murky, lusty waters of a romantic tryst with a physically handicapped woman is a milestone that few men have passed. This is usually due to small-mindedness, society's view of the handicapped as helpless, or the fact that, from a sexual perspective, the handicapped are envisioned as slovenly messes. Get over this.

Many "handi-capable" women can be sexy in their own right - especially if they are funny, charming, and merely have cerebral palsy. Cerebral palsy is a good gateway handicap and is where I recommend you begin your "make-a-wish" adventures. CP is usually a wheelchair-free zone, which is important if you live in a building with no elevator. First, you must meet a woman with CP. Make small talk and do not comment on her disease until she does. She may make a small, self-deprecating joke about her "gibbled" hand or her wonky lower torso. Simply smile with a Cheshire cat grin and acknowledge that you knew she had "special needs." After all, you're not FUCKING BLIND! Now, here is your opening. Go after her full throttle. Unleash a steady torrent of retard jokes on her that you remember from grade school.

This will make her insides tingle with glee, as she will know you have accepted her as an equal and aren't pussyfooting around her being one of God's overlooked recall models. She knows she is Christ's mistake, but you allowed her to point it out and then came back with your own brand of wit. Take this connection you've established to the next level of foreplay. She may be intelligent and funny, but you still may be turned off by her appearance. Get drinking. She can plough back as many as you - in fact, it may help her walk better. In reality, it won't help her walk better, and even doctors can't help her walk better, but feel free to insert that joke into your conversation.

Now take her out among other men. This will help her know that you value her as a person and don't consider her a detriment to society. Black men may leer at her and then give you cut-eye. This is okay - they are jealous. Once you have enough drinks in you to feel loose, take her home in a cab. Many minivans will try to pick you up. Wave the accessible-ramp cabs away in disgust at their apathy and get into a normal yellow cab. For the night, you are just two ordinary lovers and don't need government assistance.

Once you arrive at your place, you will face your biggest challenge: getting her up the stairs. This will take some time. There will be moments in this journey where she may resemble a zombie. SHE IS NOT A ZOMBIE! She is "handi-capable!" Continue to remind yourself that she is not a zombie. After the hour or two it takes to climb the stairs with this lovely young lady, you can sit her down and smoke a joint. This may be a mistake, as weed is probably not one of her prescribed meds. Also, the weed high may make you think that she is a man for a part of the evening. SHE IS NOT A MAN OR A ZOMBIE! She is handicapped and only resembles both a man and a zombie because the left side of her face is frugal with its movements.

Make out tenderly. She has not been touched for a while. Try to finger her. She may say no. Again, you will think this is because she is a man and is hiding a penis. SHE IS NOT A MAN! But if she were, you would be a closeted gay man who was attracted to handicapped people. You would be a "sicko." But you're not a "sicko" - you're high on weed. She can't have intercourse because of her CP; that's why you can't get down her pants. Play with her tits and then get her to masturbate you with her "feeling-less" left hand. This won't make you come. Actually, it will be more annoying than pleasurable. Start jacking yourself off. Then tit fuck her and bust a load of baby batter on her tits. Grab a towel and clean her up.

The next morning, be polite and tell her how to get home via subway or bus. Do not walk her downstairs - you don't have all day. Now ponder on what occurred . . . you jacked off on a "handi-capable" woman's tits. You now know what it is like to live in a prejudice-free world.

Good for you for being a gentleman.

Proper etiquette for explaining to your colleagues that you had "breast intercourse" with a handicapped woman

Allow me to say, good for you. You are a man and you do not regret the mistakes you make. You look at each and every departure from the mainstream as a learning experience. You lived through last night and made a grown woman with cerebral palsy have an experience similar to that of a blind child going to Disney World. You are a dream maker.

Many of your friends will judge you and think that you committed this act out of desperation. But no, you say; it was not boredom or semen back-up that prompted this debauchery-laden act as much as a need to understand the world better.

First, ease into the conversation. Ask your friends about the grossest "hosses" they've had the opportunity to ram their soup noodles into. You will get various responses. When one of your friends mentions banging a lady boy or an underage girl while teaching English in Thailand or Korea, you will have your opening to mention that you hooked up with what the French refer to as "la retard."

Mention that you in no way took advantage of the Jerry Lewis telethon reject. You didn't steal her off a short bus. Rather, you knew she was into it because she kept making positive noises throughout the experience.

At this point, mock the most stereotypical retarded noises you can. This will either get a laugh or a look of shock. Either way, you will have earned an organic reaction from a tale of twisted lust which most people would take to their graves with them.

That is what separates you from the peanut gallery. You have a story to tell. Stories make gentlemen. Well done, sir. If you are a politician or a religious leader, disregard all of this and pretend the entire palsy thing never happened.

In fact, if she tweets about it, block her and disavow any knowledge of the city she is in.

Proper etiquette for getting your ass kicked

Part of being a gentleman is defending honor. Sometimes it will be the honor of a woman, and sometimes it may be our own honor; either way, we may have to be involved in physical altercations at some point in our lives. There are those few people who go through life without ever being involved in a fist fight. We can call them "pussies" or blocked intellectuals. As we try to fit into this world, we will often be faced with people who are envious of us or flat-out don't like us. Then it is time to fight.

Gone are the old playground days, when we would arrange to meet up with the sandbox bully and somehow we would luckily get a few shots in before he made us lick frozen dog shit, and then we would have to go back to class with the fresh taste of dog feces on our tongues, scuffed knees, and crushed hopes. The embarrassment of losing that fight stayed with us for years and made us realize that we either had to get tougher, shield ourselves in a glass house of education, or get some really tough friends that we would do homework for. There are many reasons not to fight. You may think fighting is too mainstream due to the popularity of mixed martial arts, closeted gay behavior or the very downfall of America, but sometimes you need to stand up and take a good ass kicking. You can't run home to your parents anymore. God damn it, you're in your 30s!

First, find someone to fight. Don't pick on weak people. Avoid gingers, gangly guys, handicapped folks, blind people, homeless women (they may bleed AIDS onto you), senior citizens, and albino black folks. Also, do not go too far to the other extreme. Do not pick fights with guys that wear TAP OUT shirts in an un-ironic fashion; black people (especially in groups); tall, flexible folks; and people who are so ugly that they have nothing to lose.

The fight cannot be initiated by you.

If you do succeed in beating the enemy's ass, you may get arrested, and the cops need to know that you were defending yourself. You may have a few drinks in you and be at a bar when you get in your fight, but make sure that you have some reinforcements around. Usually a girl that is flirting can be the cause of the fight. Now, once the flirty slut has stirred the pot, you must wait until the enemy starts with you. Then go outside.

If you are in New York City, do not start the fight on a main street, as cops will show up right away and you will not get to prove your manhood before they drag you off to the Tombs for assault and disturbing the peace. Find an alley or a side street. Let him take the first punch. Do not let it connect. Then use your strength to grapple and use your weight to dominate until he taps out. If you have no defensive or grappling skills, you will find that you are now getting your ass kicked in an alley over some girl that neither of you two "wanna-be alpha males" are gonna fuck.

She is probably back in the bar flirting with more men. You are also probably about 12 punches into getting your face mangled. If you are getting your ass kicked, turtle on the ground and guard your privates, your face, your head, and whatever else you can guard. Hopefully, somebody will stop this animal from beating you to within an inch of your life. Soon it will be over. Get up and dust yourself off. Go get a drink. Do not go back to the bar in which you started the fight. That Neanderthal may still be there doing shots, looking for a second round to take out the misery he feels from never having been loved by his father. DO NOT TALK SHIT AFTER GETTING YOUR ASS KICKED! You got your ass kicked for talking shit. Keep your mouth shut.

Hopefully, a bar will let you in for a drink even though you look like you have been dragged behind a high-speed horse through rocky terrain. You look like a hooker who doesn't listen. Your friends will look at you like a bit of a loser for a while; they are justified in doing so. Hopefully, they will stay with you for a drink. Try to talk sports or something along the lines of pop culture, avoid boxing chatter.

Go home in a cab. You don't need every loser on public transit to see how badly you got your ass kicked. The judgment from one Pakistani cabbie will suffice. For the next couple of days, you may have a fat lip and a black eye. Go about your adult life feeling like the loser you are.

Do not talk shit; merely admit that you got your ass kicked in a bar fight, even though you are almost a middle-aged man. Tell the truth about the fight. Now is the time to either realize that you need to keep your mouth shut or enroll in a fighting class.

As the black eye heals, you may be able to get some pity pussy out of this situation. This should not be an impetus to getting your ass kicked again, but enjoy having your wounds licked. This has humbled you. Getting your ass kicked makes you a better gentleman.

And if you kicked the other guy's ass, you were already a fine gentleman.

Proper etiquette for doing cocaine with losers

Cocaine helped many creative people succeed in the 1980s. It has also been the subject of many documentary-type "bio-pics" as well as being a central plotline in many great Hollywood films. The best documentary on cocaine was Cocaine Cowboys, a film about how the drug changed Miami in the 80s and how the city as we know it was actually built using drug money. It also shows the violence that was associated with the importation of the drug. Where there are drugs, there is money, and where there is money, there is violence. Hollywood captured the

American cocaine boom in films like Scarface and Blow. There are other less glamorous portrayals as well. But if we learned anything from celluloid, it's that cocaine is a hell of a rush.

In 2014, cocaine is making a comeback, but it's not as mainstream as it was in the 80s. It's still around, but you have to look harder to find it. People in show business still use blow, but it's also available to the lower echelon of society via the service industry. These are people who work hard and party hard as well. These folks all think of themselves as blocked artists, and they believe that the drug will help them accomplish their dreams. They are wrong. First, you must find this "type" of people. Become a regular at a bar that has a classy façade. You can go to a dive bar, but the quality of the cocaine will be lesser than the quality in a bar where people think that they are destined for success.

Most people who work in a dive bar are lifers. They know that they are going to be stuck in the service industry long after their looks are gone. People in a flashier atmosphere still aspire to greatness. These are the losers that you want to hang out with. The hope instilled in them makes them far more desperate than the dive bar workers who have flat-out given up. This will also make the amphetamine-driven conversations much more compelling and intense.

Go to your favorite bar and have a few drinks. Once the booze has kicked in, you will feel yourself getting tired. This is when you want to subtly bring up how much you wish that you had some coke to take the edge off of the booze. Don't appear desperate or exhibit any behavior that makes you appear like a drug addict. Simply mention coke. See what the feedback is. Sooner or later, somebody at the bar will mention that they know a guy. You will have to pool your money together. Get at least a hundred bucks together. Cocaine isn't cheap, and you shall find out why shortly.

Within a drink or two, the drugs will arrive. Your acquaintance will pay his guy and then secretly pass you a bag. Go into the bathroom by yourself. Take a key and dip into the bag and do a few bumps by your lonesome in the bathroom. "Man, this is glamorous," you'll think to yourself. After a couple bumps, you'll think "OK, I'm good." You are far from good. Go take the bag back to your acquaintance. They will excuse themselves and go do a few bumps. You will worry about how many bumps they did. Did they do more than you? What weasels! Cocaine thieves! Go back to your drink. You will start to feel clear-headed and less drunk.

In about 20 minutes, you will want more cocaine; you will have to ask your drug partner for the bag again. Retreat to the restroom again. Do more blow this time; don't cheap out. Go back and give your "friend" the blow. This person is now a "friend" because you are doing blow together. He has gone from an acquaintance to a friend in the matter of an hour, all because of cocaine. The friend will go and do more blow. Soon, this bar will close. You will now think that this classy bar in which you just killed four hours is a dump. Go to another bar. Do more coke in the bathroom together. Somebody may walk in while you are both in a bathroom stall huffing rails off of a toilet paper dispenser. Don't worry - you are so cool. YOU ARE ROCK STARS!

Other people may call this behavior "gay as balls with shit on them," but you call it "partying." Soon, this bar, too, will close. Go back to one of your houses. Hopefully, by this time you have managed to pick up some slutty women who love coke as much as you do. It is probably 5 am now. Get your best friend to call his guy for more coke. His guy may not answer. "All of the coke is gone," you will exclaim. "How do we get more coke?" Call everyone you know. Around 6 am, more coke will arrive. The sun will come up soon. This is horrific. But fuck it, you're only in your 30s - you can stay up all day if you need to.

Eventually, most of this blow will disappear, and you may end up in bed with one of the slutty girls. You will try to have sex with her, but between all the booze and the cocaine, your dick will not work. Whenever you put a condom on, your penis will shrivel and become cold out of fear and numbness. You will try to slide your diminished manhood into this slutty girl with no condom. YOU ARE NOT THINKING STRAIGHT! You may get it up long enough to ejaculate mostly inside of her. MISTAKE!

Around 11 am, all the sophisticated crack-heads in your apartment will leave, and you will try to fall asleep. Good luck. You will toss and turn until about 3 pm and then may sleep awkwardly for an hour or two. Around 5 pm, you will look at yourself in the mirror and ask, "What have I become?" The answer is a loser, like all of the people you just did blow with. Within a few days, you may feel less like a worthless tool. You will vow never to do blow again. You are lying to yourself. Eventually, you may want to seek help for your occasional addiction.

Well done, degenerate gentleman.

Proper etiquette for using the "N-word" in public

Mark Twain still gets into trouble for this verbal infraction, so if you're going to use the "N-word" in public you may want to start off by utilizing the "a" ending over the "er" ending. Both are offensive and can indeed gain you likeability through looking rebellious, but you do not want to end up a "Reginald Denny" tale, so bear in mind that Twain, a famous wordsmith, still gets flak for The Adventures of Huckleberry Finn. This is a sensitive topic.

First of all, you must befriend some hip black people. These are usually people who work in the arts. Do not go up to the token black dude who works at your law firm and attempt to drop an N-bomb around him during the company golf tournament. It will merely offend him. Find some black people who actually use the word: musicians or comedians, but not actors. Black actors are way too sensitive and think that they are solving all of the world's problems by not playing thug roles, while, in fact, they're not solving anything . . . if the world's greatest black actors portrayed more thugs, Trayvon might still be alive. So avoid actors. Also avoid people who work menial jobs that they hate; they will not use the "N-word" because they still believe that everybody is calling them the "N-word" behind their backs. A gentle reminder: do not attempt use of the "N-word" with garbage men, janitors, or MTA workers.

Befriend your group of comedians or musicians and hang out with them. Do what they do. Go enjoy Nike or Adidas shoe shopping, wear skinny jeans that fit into high tops, and then get drunk with them. Have something racist happen to you collectively as a group. Be there when one of them gets called "nappy-haired," or be there when an intoxicated man leaving a club says, "Don't go in there, the place is full of niggers and spics and Jews." Hopefully, you are a spic or a Jew, because you will have just bonded through racism. You now know the plight of the black man. Some people will argue that the spics and the Jews did not live through slavery. But they did. The Jews were slaves in Egypt and "spics" were slaves during the Inquisition. Mention this to your black friends, but only in passing. Don't get all political with it and certainly don't get uppity - don't even use the term "uppity," since that term is almost as offensive as the "N-word."

Now that you have all bonded through that racist story, you are allowed to recount the story using the "N-word." Tell the story around your friends to other white people; watch as the white people look on and drool over your post-modern coolness. Watch as the white people try to repeat what you just said, and watch how your black friends look at them as if they are white devils headed for an early grave. You are now officially in the fold. Now you can use the "N-word" whenever you feel like it as long as this group of friends (or at least one of the group) is around - however, when it's one of the group instead of the entire group, this man will wonder if he has become an Uncle Tom.

You now have an "N-word" pass. Use it sparingly. Don't overindulge. Once in a while, you will overindulge; it's a tasty word. One of your black friends will tell you that "you say nigger more than a single dad in the projects after drinking his second Colt 45." This will make you think that maybe you are racist. YOU ARE NOT RACIST! You live in a post-racist society. Take a week off of the word, then come back and go drinking with your black friends. The word is back. As a gentleman, always remember: excess in moderation is the key. You have been granted a special power, so do not abuse it and do not attend any rallies where you are asked to use the word. Peace be unto you. Or, as they would say to an honorary black man, "A salaam a lakeem."

Proper etiquette for a threesome

Most men fantasize about the mythical three-way. Yet, for many, three-ways never become an easy reality. You have to work toward the ménage a trois. Sometimes threesomes happen at the most unlikely of times, so you must always be prepared for this rare form of lovemaking. In the ideal situation, you meet two female tourists from some European land, far, far away. They could be from Switzerland or Sweden or even Denmark. Try to avoid two German women, who may want to dump feces on you while spouting Nazi rhetoric and disguising their hateful acts as lovemaking.

But you fantasize about being out at a nightclub and having two models come up to you; they make out and invite you back to their hotel room. They make love to each other for a while and then exclaim in their wonky accents, "Vee are needing some cocken inside of both of us." Ideally, these women will have STD tests that are dated that day, proving that they are both clean. You would then go in and out of both of these women, satisfying them to no end until the break of dawn as they each suck their respective vaginal fluids off of your member. But realistically, most threesomes have to be paid for unless you are a Calvin Klein model or a major celebrity. So, let the dream threesome go away and deal with the true threesome.

On occasion, you may have a girl that you are banging and she has a friend who likes you and they want to bang together. If this happens, here is the way in which to handle your self. First, be grateful that you have two vaginas to deal with simultaneously; thank your girlfriend sincerely. She may try to put rules into the three-way like "you can only fuck me." THIS IS UTTER BULLSHIT! Throw that rule out the window as soon as the copulation begins. This will cost you your relationship with your chick, but so be it; better to shoot for the stars and land on the moon.

Let them start making out, sit back and masturbate until you get hard, then go in and orally pleasure both of them. Then begin by banging your regular chick very well. Then move onto the other chick. Get one girl to cup your nuts while you bang the other girl and get both of them to blow you at once. Pretend that they are a mother/daughter team who just can't get enough of you. Get one girl to guide you in and out of the other girl. Throughout all of this, remember that the woman's pleasure is tantamount. Do not come too quickly. The threesome is a bucket list kind of thing for most, so keep your wits about you.

When you have all come and are in a sticky mess on the bed, get up, light a smoke, and share it among the three of you. Once your girl's friend leaves, you may now break up with your girl. During the breakup, remind her that she wanted to do this more than you did. It's a lie, but it may save the relationship somewhere down the road. This is usually as good as a three-way with two chicks can get. It's messy when you're in a relationship.

Now for the other option, at which many of you may turn up your noses in disgust: the three-way with you, a woman, and your buddy. This type is easier to organize and has much less fallout. Find a skank who looks like she wants to have two cocks in her at the same time. These women can be found in pubs, on craigslist, or even in the streets of most metropolitan areas. Be good buddies with whoever the other guy is. Don't get trapped into one of those "would you like to bang my wife?" scenarios. Usually, these couples are creepy, and the man may very well try to bang you while you're not looking. You don't want to have to deal with this kind of unwanted ass rape. So keep it in the friend zone with the guy. Take the girl to wherever - your place, his place, or her place.

Once you arrive at a location, shit will get a bit messy and you may have to throw your moral compass out the window. You will have to swap saliva via the girl's mouth, so don't be prudish. You and your buddy don't have to make out or even touch, but a woman only has so many orifices and you and your friend will have to share and share alike. You should both kiss the woman passionately (at different times). She will go back and forth blowing you mutually. You should both go down on her at different points. Try to do this prior to one of you fucking her or you will either taste condom or your friend's cock remnants and the bleach-like scent of jism. Then one of you may enter her while the other gets blown. Then swap. Have a lot of condoms around as you may want to go from banging back to receiving head depending on how hot the girl is and how long you actually want this to last. Don't be greedy over the pussy or the mouth. Switch it up. SHARING IS CARING!

If you decide to do double penetration and get her ass involved, this has to be carefully planned. One of you may lie underneath the female part of the equation and the other may try to enter her asshole slowly. Only do this if you have good lower body strength; otherwise, your legs may buckle and your balls will crush your friend's balls, sending all four balls into your respective stomach areas. This will rid you both of your erections. If only your erection disappears and your friend gets hard, he may be gay, and this whole three-way may all be a sham for him to get balls deep inside of you. In that case, logic will take over and you will look for the best way to get out of this scenario. That will ruin the enjoyment. So hopefully, you both get soft and then decide that double penetration was not a good idea.

Go back to the faithful spit-roasting position, you in her mouth, him in her puss and then swap until you both come. Afterwards, be polite to the woman until she leaves. You and your friend may have an odd moment where you gaze into each other's eyes. Change the subject quickly. Have a beer and bro out. You have just strengthened your friendship and now can always have a secret that your friend will take to his grave after he gets married.

If you have a threesome with two other men, this chapter is not for you; please go see the play or the film Rent.

Proper etiquette for recovering from a birthday hangover

If you are living life appropriately, you will still have major blowouts even as you age. You will be faced with the responsibility of having stuff to do after these blowouts and you will have to deal with the fact that you cannot handle adult responsibilities some days. You may wake up at 41 years of age and realize that it is your birthday. You drink a bottle of Zinfandel (red, not pink) by yourself in the daytime as you sit on the roof smoking and tanning. Then you go out to some kind of birthday event that you organized since you have so few friends who actually give a shit about you and because you are single, which usually makes you happy, but on birthdays you are painfully reminded of how alone you are. You eat "s'mores" and cake and deep-fried lollipops and then you probably drink more booze; a combo of red wine, high-end scotch, and lemon drop shots because you are too womanly for real shots.

Then you go to another bar, where you smoke a joint with some hippie chick, a rare find in this day and age. She gives you shotgun hits because she probably has bronchitis or pneumonia, being a dirty hippie, and you prefer not to share a joint with her trash can of a mouth. After drinking some more, you take your artsy friend, who is a guitar act comedian, and the hippie chick home in a cab. You will want to stop at a bodega and buy two types of ice cream, birthday candles, a six pack of Heineken, two types of M and M's, one banana (for the hippie chick to get her in the phallic mood), and a pregnancy test.

You will probably forget to purchase condoms. Don't worry about it. You should have some at home. You'd better. If not, you have a pregnancy test. YOU ARE AN IDIOT FOR BUYING THAT! Then, when you get back to your place, have beers and ice creams. You will probably not finish the beers because the ice cream is too sweet. Your artsy friend probably has some very speedy cocaine in his pocket. Do a bit of it. Just a little bit. A bump, two bumps maximum. Remember this is not cocaine-fest 2014; this is just to take the edge off of the booze. You know how you get when you get all hyped on blow - your dick gets colder and angrier than a black Alaskan.

After the ice cream, have an awkward threesome with your artsy buddy who probably looks like Matisyahu with severe autism. Let him eat out the hippie chick, because even though she has a great body, her bush is a mess that is paying posthumous tribute to Janis Joplin. IF YOU WANTED A MOUTH FULL OF PUBES YOU WOULD LICK THE FLOOR OF A BLACK BARBERSHOP! Bushy beast! Let her blow you until you come. She probably already blew your friend and swallowed his artsy Brooklynesque jism before you, so do not make out with her. If you do make out with her, don't ever admit to it or write about it.

Then you will all go to sleep in the same bed. You will feel like John Lennon and Yoko Ono except there will be a third wheel, which is you; the Yoko Ono person is not Asian and you have no idea what her name is. Call her miss or madam in a joking manner to get through the night. She may ask for water on several occasions; give it to her. She swallowed two loads already, for Christ's sake, and you don't even know her name. A little tap water is the least you can do.

Wake up at noon. Feel like you should bang her but then realize that your friend is still there. Now you are feeling weird about being this "rapey" at noon. Leave them alone; let her blow him. Go clean up your filthy apartment. Then lie around and drink coffee and smoke out the window. Now you will get horny. Send your artsy friend out for breakfast sandwiches and to get the hippie chick something with avocado; hippie chicks love green shit. While your friend goes out, fuck the hippie on your couch in front of the windows so all the people in the projects can watch you slamming some afternoon delight. Black people like watching white people fuck - they find it exotic. Pull out, take the condom off and then come down her throat. She will be coughing most of the day from all the strange semen she drank, mixed with her bronchitis or pneumonia. Avoid catching this.

Breakfast will arrive shortly after your two-minute fuck session. Eat half of your sandwich and then tell those losers that you need to write and take a nap. They will leave, and he will get back on the subway with his guitar. They may talk on the way out. Aren't you glad you are at home and don't have to go anywhere? The cab ride was worth the 35 bucks last night. Now that they're gone, you realize that you have no intention of napping. Smoke more and drink some coffee, text your ex-fiancé, and try to booty call a fat chick for later on.

The fat chick will not fall for coming over to watch Pain and Gain starring the Rock; she will ask you to go out to a movie. DO NOT FALL FOR HER TRICKS! SHE IS A SLOB AND ONLY DESERVES TO BE SEEN IN PRIVATE. LIKE POLLUTED LAKE WATER, SHE IS NOT FOR PUBLIC CONSUMPTION. If you have greasy food, eat some. If not, you will need to go out to get some. Have a beer, or two, fuck it . . . it's still your birthday. Order pizza later and get out of the house for a bit or depression will take over. Scrub your dick in the sink. You screwed a hippie harder than the cops did when they took back Wall Street.

Take Advil if you have some. Remember this for next year.

Proper etiquette for being a boyfriend

Do not confuse this chapter with being locked into monogamy. Being a boyfriend and being monogamous are often one and the same, but they are not necessarily the same. It is nice to believe that when you are a boyfriend to a woman that you are going to be in a monogamous three-hole relationship, but it doesn't have to be that way. My belief is that until you say "I love you," everything in the realm of side-pussy is still fair game. Some people may not agree with this perfect, realistic world-view; we call those people "most women." However, until you are locked down into the temporary façade that is love and monogamy, here are some tips on being a good boyfriend.

You will actually need to have a talk with the girl that you are fucking regularly so that you know you are in fact her boyfriend now. Otherwise, you may be playing guitar outside of a woman's window for no reason after an argument. This line has to be perfectly drawn in the sand. There can be no illusory concepts here. Either you are her boyfriend or you aren't. You may have had some experiences where you did not clearly draw this line and you were pushed into the friend zone by a girl whom you had already banged and treated to dinner. This is a waste of assets and should be avoided. Why would you want to be a boyfriend? Place to stay, extra money when you need it, free drinks at the bar where your "girlfriend" works. These are all good reasons.

So you will have to sit down with the woman you've been courting and talk. Usually women do this, but we are gentlemen. Mention that you enjoy her company and ask how she sees you together. She will ask if you are sleeping with anybody else. Lie and tell her that you haven't been with anybody since you met her. She will believe this lie. Then she will ask, "Am I your girlfriend?" You will say "It certainly looks that way." BOOM!! Now you have a girlfriend. Prepare for the side-pussy offers to begin rolling in. Women can smell the commitment in your very presence. Now you will have to do boyfriend stuff with your girlfriend. This involves having her make you hangover breakfasts while you lay on the couch watching meaningless TV. This is a good thing. Your girlfriend, however, is trying to fatten you up to take you off the market. DO NOT LET THIS HAPPEN! Keep your gym regimen strong. Attempt to maintain some semblance of abs.

You will have dinners together. Try to make sure that, after the initial courting phase, your girlfriend pays for most of these dinners. During some of these dinners, you will have to meet her friends. You will want to fuck some of her friends. DO NOT ACT ON THIS IMPULSE! In a few months or a few years after you are broken up, you may bang her friends, but not now. This is frowned upon in polite circles. Most of her friends will be idiots. She may have some guy friends. They will fall by the wayside shortly. You will have to meet her family members. Most of them are probably half-retards. Put up with them. Try to find some kind of common ground on which you can carry a conversation with these Down-syndrome Neanderthals she calls relatives.

You will probably have to talk sports with the male members of the family and equal wages with the female members of the family. If she has brothers, they will hate you because you are routinely putting your penis inside of their sister. They used to dream about fucking their own sister because they are hillbillies. They may pretend to like you because you are making their sister happy. This is temporary. They have a deep, dark disdain for you and wish that their sister were dating a black guy so that they could talk basketball and casually use the "N-word" around him when drinking. Be on your best behavior when you are around her family. They may be able to do something for you financially.

You will have to go to movies with your girlfriend. Once in a while, it will be a film of her choosing. It will be awful. Sit through it and then act like you deserve a blowjob or anal sex afterwards. She will respond accordingly. You will realize that women cry a lot more than men. She will cry throughout your relationship. PRETEND THAT YOU CARE! Hold her and let her cry. Girlfriends do not want you to solve their problems; they just want you to hear their problems!

You will have to argue with your girlfriend on occasion. It will be exhausting, but it is something that you have to do. If you win the argument, you have lost in the long run. Let her win a few arguments or at least think that she has won. After arguments, you will feel angry. This is a good time to cheat on her. Make sure that your cheat is cleverly concealed and do not get caught. You will feel better. Remember, you haven't said "I love you" yet, so technically it isn't even cheating; that being said, pretend that it never happened and lie to yourself about it.

You may have to go on a vacation with your girlfriend. You will wish that you were golfing or fishing with your friends instead. Don't mention this out loud. Merely drink your way through the vacation. You will have to listen to your girlfriend bitch about work and her co-workers; pretend that you are interested and that you know what she does for a living. It is probably something involving the Internet.

You will be expected to have sex with your girlfriend regularly. You are bored with having sex with her by now. Do it anyway. A good thing about having a girlfriend is that once you have been together for a while, you don't have to impress her any more in the sack. By now, you have both realized that you are sick of each other. She may accidentally say she loves you out of fear of being alone. You can either say, "I love you too," or say, "That's nice." Either way, the boyfriend phase is over. You will now have to be serious about each other or go your own way. GO YOUR OWN WAY! You already proved you can be a boyfriend. You don't need to take this to the next level of co-habitation followed by engagement, followed by marriage, followed by becoming a divorce statistic.

Get out while there is still getting to be gotten.

Proper etiquette for dealing with erectile dysfunction without acknowledging it to your partner

Men . . . we have manhood. Our manhood is often exhibited in our sex drive and our ability to act on our sex drive. We recall fondly our earlier years, which were filled with sexual desires that were fulfilled on a regular basis. We would fantasize about vaginas, and then one day we got vaginas - many vaginas for some of us, fewer vaginas for others of us. We drank from the overflowing cup that was "woman juice." Years of plotting and planning to get their pants off finally paid off. Because we are men, we strive to conquer. At one point or another, we found ourselves sick of running around like stray dogs looking for the next hole to hump, and we settled down for a while. We became monogamous. We liked the fact that we were only with one woman and that we had grown up. We were gentlemen who had moved past their insecure days.

Then we realized that we needed out of this situation. We were being emotionally strangled by the purveyor of one vagina. So once again, we gave up security and ventured out into the crazy, unknown, vaginal wilderness. But we were older now and jaded by pussy. We had seen hundreds of them, and now it took us more to get turned on. We spent years abusing our manhood, and our manhood had become a grizzled vagina veteran. Our dick had heard all the "queefs," smelled all the smells, and seen all the different types, and it was now much more specific in what it was looking for. Our manhood had become site-specific. We were too used to jacking off to exactly what we craved in the moment. We expect a fat Asian woman dressed as a Catholic school girl to just appear with glasses on, ready to take our loads. Sex requires more work than that.

So, tirelessly, we venture forth; looking for that next kink that gets us aroused. Bear in mind, this isn't the old days. Women may be attracted to us in droves, but we are bored. Here's how to get your "mojo" back.

Go out on a date. Or go out to a bar. Meet a woman. Don't make it your first priority, but make it an "up there" kind of thing. You want to have sex tonight! As an older gentleman, if you put that out into the universe it will come back to you. Have some drinks with this woman. Sit down and talk to her. Actually talk. Forget about sex for this moment in time. As an older, distinguished gentleman, do not be afraid to take her into the friend zone. In fact, that is what you want to do.

The no-friend zone theory was set up by young "30-somethings" who needed trends to talk about, and the friend zone is still a fuck-friendly zone when you are in your late 30s/early 40s. This is due to the fact that both parties involved have learned that it's more fun to fuck somebody that you get along with than somebody you don't. We have also learned that there are fewer options out there. So we are less choosy. Sit and talk about whatever comes honestly to you. Avoid the topic of sex. If you talk to a woman about sex right away, you will not get sex unless she is a total whore, and that should not be a turn-on to you. Total whores have pussies that look like they may have been practice tracks for dirt bike races.

So avoid the topic of sex unless you are with a total whore, but if you are with a total whore, you should stop drinking soon because you'll have to get up early and pay 100 bucks to go visit a doctor. If, however, you live in Canada, you may keep drinking, as health care will cover most of your STDs, so consider that 100 dollars disposable income which can be spent on booze in the present moment. Soon, you may feel the evening moving toward sex. Here are the problems you must now encounter; you have had too much to drink, talking to this woman for this long made her less attractive, and you know that you are so jaded by sex that you are nearly impotent.

There is one solution to all of these problems: getting a dick pill. Dick pills were invented accidentally by doctors attempting to cure heart disease, but they serve us quite well. Usually you require a prescription or a doctor to get legitimate dick pills. These pills include but are not limited to Viagra, Cialis, and Levitra. You may know somebody who is a doctor or who has a prescription. If this is the case, then you may have hit them up at some point for a sample of these pills. And if that is the case, you may have one in your wallet. If that is the case, excuse yourself, go to the restroom, and pop the pill with some tap water.

The pill bottle's label may state "do not take with alcohol" . . . THE PILL BOTTLE DON'T KNOW YOU! Take the pill if you have it. If not, you will need to find a reason to run to a convenience store/deli/bodega and get an over-the-counter dick pill.

These dick pills are not as safe as the prescription dick pills, but they do work. Common examples of these knock-offs are Samurai X, Existenz, and other weirdo names. Do not get the "healthy" herbal pills, as they are yohimbe shit. You need a chemical boost. Take the pill quickly and return to the woman. Do not think about taking the pill or about sex. See, as the drug kicks in, it will respond to wherever the blood is rushing. So if you are thinking, blood rushes to your brain, and your face will turn red. This will almost look like an allergic reaction. This will raise some questions from your lady friend like "Are you allergic to my pussy?" Questions are not what we want now, as questions will make us think more and will drive more blood to our faces, making us redder than a freshly used tampon.

GET OUT OF THIS BAR! Pay your tab and leave. Get her to touch your penis as soon as you get into a cab. This will get the blood away from your face and back to your penis. Go home and bang her multiple times. She will be shocked at your prowess and your stamina. Dick pills allow you to get hard mere moments after ejaculation. The girl will ask why you're so turned on. Lie and tell her it is because of her. This will make her more turned on.

You will have a great night of sex. You will wake up with a painful erection. Hopefully, she is still there. Go at it again. She had great sex. You performed well, but you know that you are living a lie. This girl will clearly want to see you again since she hasn't been fucked like this since she cheated on her ex-husband with a Jamaican drummer from a calypso band. You may see her again, but just know that you will be expected to perform like this all the time. You cannot.

These dick pills take a voracious toll on your heart and your health. Use them sparingly. If you form a relationship with this woman, you will be screwed down the road. You can never admit to dick pills.

If you stop using them, you will be a shadow of the man you once were, and this woman will leave you for a new dick-pill-taking liar. Use dick pills on special occasions, and only bang the women you bang with dick pills on two separate nights. Now go see a doctor and get your heart checked.

Proper etiquette for dating three or four women at once

We can't all look like or even live the life of James Bond, but we will go through phases in our lives when we are so creatively inspired that women pick up on it and we are able to be what the French refer to as "polyamorous." This is a dream come true. We get to be with multiple women who, in combination, give us all we need. Cumulatively, these women go from being mere holes to filling all the holes in our own lives. We are smart enough when this happens to know that one woman does not a complete life make. We are well-dressed cavemen, so indulge.

First, you must find three or four women who are open-minded enough to let you put your penis inside of them. You can meet these women while online, through friends, while on a bus, on the street; wherever. Just meet them. Get their phone numbers. Call them or text them. Make arrangements to go out. Do not sleep with them right away, or sleep with them right away - it doesn't really matter. You are a stallion, and you make your own rules. You don't live by Steve Harvey's emasculatory dating advice on what women want. How the hell does he know what women want - he doesn't even know how to buy a suit that fits. Now one of the keys here is to be honest with all of these women. Let them know that you are fucking more than one woman. This will turn them on. They will see your hunter mentality at work. You will be fucking around the clock.

Ensure that you schedule these women appropriately. For example, if one is a good drinker, you want to be with her later in the evening; if one has bad morning breath, you want to catch her mid-afternoon; if one makes a good breakfast, you may want to sleep over; and if one is rich, you may want to drop the other three and move in with her. All of these women should have various qualities. You are after all, living a dream. So don't limit yourself. You may want to have one fat girl, one skinny girl, one "blowjobby" girl, and another fat girl. Keeping the fat girls around ensures that you will be able to get your rocks off in the most bizarre of ways, while the other two girls are for public appearances.

Don't get me wrong - you can take the fat girls out in public, but only if they are financially sponsoring you. The fat girls will be very happy that you're fucking them, unless they're the fat girls with tattoos and a hipster attitude, in which case they may feel as if they are doing you a favor. THEY ARE NOT! YOU ARE A STUD! THEY ARE FAT! We do not live in Rembrandt's time period anymore. Fat women can be loved, but it must be realized that they are fat because of lack of discipline, not big bones, thyroids, or their popularity as chick comedians. Not to say that fat women are worth less than normal women; they're not, especially if we were in a plane crash; the fat women would be worth far more if we had to eat them in the mountains.

Don't answer calls from any of the girls when you are out with one of the other girls. For even though the women know that you are not being exclusive, they still get upset easily. Also, do not drunk text, as you may send the wrong text to the wrong girl at the wrong time, and this will cause issues. Also, be careful when sober texting. Sooner or later, one of the girls, if not all three of the girls, will want you to commit exclusively to them. This is the beginning of the end.

Save yourself, pick one girl that you think you can stay with for a while, and get the fuck out of Dodge. By this point, you can throw out all of your condoms and know that you fought the good fight. Some of the women will be upset that you left them in the dust; these will probably be the two fat women and the woman who wouldn't swallow. Well played. Now enjoy monogamy for a few months until it all implodes, your morality crumbles, and you realize that you are now part of the problem with the world.

Proper etiquette for going through a dry spell

None of us want to be lonely, decrepit creatures and live without the nurturing yet occasionally nagging touch of a woman. However, unless you are one of God's few George Clooney types (and I bet even Clooney saw some "pussyless" days in his Facts of Life heights), you will encounter a dry spell or 2,000 in your life. There are ways to deal with it. Sometimes women do not come to us because we do not believe ourselves to be attractive. Do not be fooled; when you have stuff going on and are creative and busy, you will have to beat off "poon" with a stick - figuratively, of course, unless you live in Africa or some less-developed areas of Canada where "bitch-sticking" is still in its early days of sport. Yet dry spells happen, and they are not to be taken lightly.

Stinky axe wound love will know us again, but in the meantime, here is how to deal. First, fight every human impulse you have and DO NOT RAPE! It is illegal, and women don't take this evidence of misogyny well. Rape has gone so far that women and liberals get upset about rape jokes. They have even coined the term "rape culture." It's a little bleeding heart since there is no real culture to rape (unless you count the swabbing which occurs post-rape in the DNA kit - BOOM - rape comedy); there is no culture, no rape parades, no rape food or drink (cranberry and vodka and roofies - BOOM - more rape comedy).

But seriously, folks . . . rape is wrong. There was a time when rape was accepted, but this was a long time ago and was called college (BOOM -that's three). Seriously, rape was okay with Vikings, but that time is gone. You are a gentleman; you need not rape. You only need to have the Internet. Whenever you see a woman you think of sexually, do not approach her and risk more rejection throwing fuel on the fire of your loser-y dry spell; merely make a mental image of her and go home and rub one out finding someone who resembles her on YouPorn or RedTube. Do this with women you've always imagined being with, even if you haven't seen them recently. Jack off a lot, eat sandwiches, and nap. Do not jack off into socks as you are not 12 years old. Waste toilet paper instead. We live in a nearly paperless society, but there is still no replacement for paper jerk towels.

Jack off more, eat more sandwiches, and then nap more. Sooner or later, you will tire of being a semenless slug living on turkey breast, Swiss cheese, and mayo on light rye. You will be well rested from napping. You will start jogging again and will get in shape so you don't have to be a celibate manatee. Or you will get so depressed by your body's come-free clock being overfed that you will go out drinking in the only kind of bar that will admit your sunless carcass: a PUB, and you will hook up with a female version of yourself and have sloppy, fat, unprotected, "consensual" intercourse. Welcome back to the game, playa. Aren't you glad you didn't rape? Yes, you would have gotten to know "affection," but the Huffington Post would have ostracized you.

Now use the smell of the woman on your groin as a pheromone to attract more women, trap a wealthy one, and then move to Arizona and buy a mansion for 100 grand, as the family who built their dreams into that home weep endlessly and carry out all they have left in cardboard boxes. Because hey, it's not our fault the real estate market collapsed while we were going through a dry patch.

Well done, gentleman/new homeowner.

Proper etiquette for paying for sex

I'm not going to claim that all men get to a point where we need to pay for sex, or even that we all get to a point where we want to pay for sex. Is it necessary that man pays for sex? I mean it is not a necessary or sufficient condition of life from a philosophical standpoint that man pays for sex, but does it make things more interesting???? Damn straight. Now there are several ways that we can pay for sex, and I don't mean in the hackneyed BET comic way: "Every time we be taking a woman out for dinner, that be like her being a ho. Ladies, you all hos, but you all got different price tags. Also, give it up for the ladies, God's most beautiful inventions." Then, they wait for applause and continue: "But seriously, ladies, if you ain't gonna be selling the pussy then why it look like a credit card swiper???? Peace, I'm out, bring the troops back safe, God bless all y'all!"

Girlfriends and dates are girlfriends and dates; they are not hookers. So here are the modern-day options for paid sex: street-walkers (real hookers), online escort services, erotic masseuses, and the ads in the backs of newspapers. There are also hookers who work in bars and casinos, but those hos are overpriced and too pretty. We want our hookers to have a bit of "street gristle" on them so we know that we can do better in the real world. You do not want a hooker to be the hottest girl you have ever had because this will ruin your will to live, and you will fully buy into the capitalist model that has destroyed the American economy.

Some people like to know exactly what their hookers are going to look like. However, this is never truly possible. If you go online, the pictures may be from before their pimp busted their lips, or the photo will probably not show the herpes simplex b outbreak. Newspapers may have photos, but they, too, may be inaccurate or dated. Most erotic masseuses don't post pictures because they may lose their legit nursing jobs. Streetwalkers are the closest you can get to seeing what your investment actually looks like, but street lights are much more forgiving than 60-watt indoor bulbs are, so they, too, may be hiding secrets and years with makeup and bruises. So accept the fact that most of the time your hooker will be a surprise and embrace it.

However you get the hooker to your door, she will arrive later than you expected. Hookers are busy getting filled with cock all around the city, so be patient. When your hooker arrives, answer the door fully clothed. Be polite. Many hookers have been victimized by the "rape culture" and are aware that you may have four guys hiding in your bathroom with baseball bats and a chainsaw waiting to tear them into pieces and feed those pieces to a Rottweiler. So make sure she feels welcome. Be alone when the hooker arrives. Sometimes, these pros have a biker waiting outside in a van. Let him wait. You have paid for this meth addict to be romantic with your lonely self. By the way, pay her immediately.

Once the whore is paid, she will let her man know that she has the dough. That is truly all he cares about. Now you are free to threaten her well being. He will now drive away and leave you with his bottom bitch. Now this will not be a sex free-for-all. If you want a BBBJ (bareback blowjob), or Greek (ass fucking), or a golden shower (getting pissed on, you sick fuck), you need to discuss all these things prior to payment, as these are all hooker up-sells, much like guacamole and extra cheese are at a Mexican restaurant. Do not get overly rough with your ho, but make sure that you get your hour's worth. Hookers vary in price from 10 dollars to 2,500 dollars per hour. No matter what you paid, you are entitled to a full hour. Do not feel like less of a man just because you paid for sex. Get your hour's worth. Hookers are usually good at sex. They know tricks to get you to finish quickly. DO NOT FINISH QUICKLY! Get your goddamned money's worth. Try all the positions you can. Hold off on coming. Go through as many condoms as you like. You may think that you will get to come more than once in an hour. YOU ARE WRONG! She will try to leave once you come and you cannot chain her up and hold her hostage. That is frowned upon.

Also, make sure that you have not done a ton of cocaine or boozed too heavily prior to your hooker arriving. Nothing feels worse than dropping 200 bucks and having a professional stare at your flaccid dick for an hour while you talk about how much you miss your ex. Some hookers may fall in love with you, especially if you are in a small town and you present them with the opportunity to get out of that town. They may tell you that you don't need a condom. DO NOT LISTEN TO THEM! Such a woman is a whore, both literally and figuratively. Wrap your dick in latex and keep your eyes on this crafty wench. She may try to get pregnant with your seed and pop out an AIDS baby. Last thing you need is a pregnant hooker; pregnant sluts are bad enough.

Sexually speaking, hookers are okay with most positions. Some hookers dislike doggy style, even though they realize that it will make you finish quicker; however, they may have been raped in this position by a football team, so respect their wishes. When you finish, scrub down in the sink with soap and water. If you licked her tits, brush your teeth and use mouthwash. If you ate her pussy, you may be gay and need an intervention; that is hooker cunt, weirdo!! Do not leave any valuables near the filthy whore. She may steal even if she is not a transvestite crack-head. Let the hooker out and double-lock the doors. Look at yourself in the mirror, and know that you are the king of the world.

If this hooker experience was good, you can go online and rate the ho on various chat-rooms and websites; if she was horrible like a girl I got in Ottawa once, make sure you tell everybody that she sucked and was a rip-off who got tired of sucking dick four minutes in and asked me to finish myself off. BAD WHORE! Ottawa hookers are shit.

However, if you have a good hooker, word of mouth does wonders for their business. So I'd like to take this opportunity to send a shout out to AAA Escort in Fredericton, New Brunswick. They were always extraordinary, with the exception of one toothless native woman (they lied and told me that she was Brazilian). Their rate was 120 dollars an hour, and I was usually very satisfied. Try them out, if you are ever in Fredericton, New Brunswick on fishing or logging business!

Proper etiquette for having an online presence

There was a time when only sketchy people and "kiddy-diddlers" would maintain an online presence. They had to do this because there was no other confidential form of picking up fat girls or kids they wanted to fuck at the time. Then along came shows like Dateline MSNBC with "To Catch a Predator." This put a chink in the armor of many pedophiles and made chubby chasers be wary about whom they were trying to pick up online.

Now let me take this opportunity to mention that the Internet may have been started with the best of intentions: some kind of wisdom-instilling mega-machine that would speed up the intelligence of the populace and enable humanity to operate on the highest level so that we could communally engage in some kind of peaceful oneness. But in reality, the Internet is used to fuck people, to meet people to fuck, to stalk people you want to meet, or to jack off so that you don't have to go through the trouble of meeting new people. Let's face it; not meeting people is a whole lot easier than meeting people. But as a gentleman, you want to use the Internet to both meet new people and to expand your business. Money, fame and power are on the to-do lists of all gentlemen, and clearly the Internet helps achieve all of these things. Look at all of the talentless, socially autistic retards who have gained famed and notoriety because of social networking sites. When push comes to shove and these people are actually hurled into the limelight to do what they profess they can do, we often see that they are much better hidden away; they are a pill better taken in 140-character doses than in four-minute sets on late-night TV. But behind the glowing veil of the Internet, these people rocket to fame.

So you must find a way to represent what you do online and be able to back it up in person (most bloggers are incapable of this). You want to keep your presence simple. A website that lists all of your major accomplishments, shows your integrity, provides both video and written evidence of how great you are (from real newspapers, not blogs with inexperienced writers who are in fact aspiring comics/humans), the contact info of your team . . . you must have a team. If people can get to you too easily, you are desperate. Have at least one manager per country if not per coast, have several agents that represent varying aspects of your gentlemanliness, have a publicist (have several as you will fire many of them), a public appearance booker, a website PR person, a legal team (this can be just one lawyer, but have them be American - even though the Canadian and British legal systems are better rounded than the US system, the US still believes its justice system is infallible), and then in very small print, you may have an email address for yourself.

This email address that is just for you will probably only be used by (1) stalkers, (2) women who want your seed inserted near their cervixes, and (3) people who want to undercut your actual price by avoiding dealings with your agent. The fourth possible option for this email address is people with whom you went to high school. Usually, these people would contact you via Facebook, but you are not on Facebook because you are a gentleman. Fuck Facebook and fuck the mainstream. Gentlemen are old school. You cave where you have to, but Facebook is not the caving point. You may have a fan page set up by your online publicist if you have enough fame to justify a fan page. But other than that, stay off Facebook and stay in demand.

Our own website is run by your web designer who works for you. You only need one "like" on that site, and that "like" is your own personal "like." Next step; do not go on MySpace unless the year is 2004 and you are a time-traveler. If it is 2004, you will see a man named Dane Cook. Stop him, by any means necessary. Then stop all the comedians that make fun of him between 2005 and 2012. Then stop Louis CK from releasing a new hour every year; he has overextended himself artistically. Okay, time traveler, back to now.

Myspace used to be cool, but in 2014, it's not. Lavalife was a good dating site to find women to bang, but better sites have come along . . . tinder, match.com, etc. Use these, but only discreetly. Do not go on JDate, even if you are Jewish. You will meet people who know your parents, and then your parents will find out how sketchy you are. So, thus far, you have your own website and some fuck-sites. Get on Twitter. It's easy enough and it can help put asses in seats for live events. You can also meet some people who are good from a networking point of view. Sign up for Instagram, but never use it. Go on Vine and use Vine merely to enhance your Twitter experience. Avoid the new fads like Pheed, unless you know about them first-hand.

Whenever you hear an "artist" talking solely about a new site, you may write this person off as a talentless cunt. The personal website is still the best type of online presence. Other people will tell you that you need to do everything online. These people have the time to do that because they are never creating and they are trying to pursue fame for the sake of fame. Fame is over-rated. Wealth is under-rated. Chase neither of these things online because you will end up giving your bank account info to a Nigerian banker and your Twitter password to an "agent" based in South Florida.

At times, you will want to write tweets that are subversive, intellectual, and full of venom. Make sure you're sober when you do these things. Always make sure you're sober when you're posting online. Things can come back to haunt you. The Internet is not a conversation between two people. It is a conversation with the world, or at least a conversation with the 311 followers you have. Be safe out there, gentlemen, and remember not to fuck too far out of your age bracket on either side while online dating . . . you may end up with your aunt or your adopted nephew.

Proper etiquette for going out for coffee with a large woman that you thought was attractive (before you masturbated)

First, you must meet this woman when your adrenaline is pumping. You have to be feeling good about yourself. Feeling good about yourself will convince you that you can date far below your dating bracket. You will be in a place of confidence when you are on the hunt and believe that looks don't matter, because you are your own man and you define yourself by who you are, not whom you date. Get her number and then set something up for a few days later. Text her in a day or two and make arrangements for coffee; you would just invite her over for sex, but that is what hookers are for. Who are you to take work away from good working girls? Set up a time for 3:30. Then text her at 2 and tell her that you're running late because of the gym. She won't understand. This slob probably hasn't seen the inside of a gymnasium since third grade when she tried to climb a rope and ended up with a participation badge.

She may not answer the text for some time, as she is probably throwing up from nerves. She wants to look her best for you. Good for her. Maybe if she thought like that whenever she passed a mirror, this wouldn't be such a "to-do." She'll finally answer your text and say "no problem" or something that she finds witty in three or less letters. Drop some sex hints over text, such as "I'd be there earlier, but this leather g-string needs washing." She will probably respond "LOL" to that and she probably did actually laugh out loud, as there is not much happiness in this woman's life. Meet her in a coffee shop that is a little bit out of the way so you don't bump into anyone you know. For the most part, you are considered a winner among your peers, and you don't need them to see you showing up at a hip coffee bar with a woman who looks like she was saved by Greenpeace.

So take her somewhere off the beaten path (although any place she is at, the path must have been beaten to get to, she is HUGE). When you walk in, give her a hug and a little peck on the cheek. This does not necessarily look romantic to the public, but it feels romantic to her. The public will think things like "maybe he's gay," "maybe they're old high school friends," or "she must be his sugar mama." They will not think that you are together. Offer to get her a coffee or a tea. No snacks for Miss Diabetes 2014 just yet. The sexy barista woman will perceive you as a kindly soul. "Who is this man to do this white whale a favor?" She will not say that, but you can feel it in the way she makes your cappuccino. Go sit down and take interest in what this woman says. Do not comment on how cute her eyes are; that is the only positive thing you can find right now, so save it.

This woman will tell you about her horror stories of dating online. Of course they are horror stories - she probably didn't enclose a body shot in her profile, and she probably had three friends hold her chins out of camera range during the photo. Let me tell you how online dating actually works for big women. Men take them to bars, drink heavily to deal with how big these women are, and come onto the women; then the women think all men want to fuck them. "Yes; all intoxicated men want to fuck you, and so do most black men. You are the weakest gazelle. You are a Last Call Lucy. Now move on with the story." DO NOT SAY THAT ALOUD! She will mention how many roommates she has and how she moved here from somewhere in Texas and how she loves Texas.

This girl across the table from you, sipping a sweet tea, has already pictured a life together with you. Here come the questions: "Have you ever been married?" "Do you have any kids?" "Do you want kids?" Jesus Christ, lady, this is coffee, let your 40 McNuggets from lunch digest before we start talking future. Then she may hit you with "I know you were engaged before." This means that in between bites of Subway's new rib sub, this pig took the time to cyber stalk you. Tell her about your engagement, why you broke it off, and be polite about your ex. After all, your ex may have been crazy and ambitious, but at least men other than amputees and food bloggers would hit on her.

Don't ask about her ex, as clearly it will drive her to eating more. In fact, judging from her appearance, she may have eaten her ex. Then she will bring up how she goes to a Presbyterian church, thus managing to bring past relationships, her false God, and children all into a first chat. You may wonder why she lives in New York City. No doubt she thinks Woody Allen is a sandwich on her Weight Watcher's menu and Simon and Garfunkel are types of mayonnaise. You may want to say, "You are grossing me out, let's get out of here before more people comment on how weird we look sitting together." AGAIN, DO NOT SAY THIS ALOUD!

Go for a walk with King Kong Bundy's sister. She will look confused at first; you'll have to guide her, telling her "one foot, then the next." Walking is new to this creature that had to blowtorch herself off the couch to get here. Make sure that you go up some stairs so you can watch her be winded. This will humble her. She will inform you that she is unemployed and is living on unemployment. This makes it clear that her hope for today was for you to bust a load inside of her, knock her up, and take her back to Texas whilst financially supporting a baby that wouldn't show up on an ultrasound due to this mountain's pure mass.

Hug her and say goodbye. Tell her that you had fun and that you will call her soon. She will go home and masturbate with an undercooked chicken leg. You will go home and look up chubby red heads on your favorite porn site. When you come inside of a paper towel today, that will be one of the smartest loads you ever spent.

See, sometimes dates end exactly the way we want them to.

The proper etiquette for when you think you may have an STD (or when you actually have an STD)

Nowadays, 97 percent of us have STDs thanks to HPV, which was invented by the Illuminati to be used on white people to destroy ovaries and thereby shrink the white population one generation at a time. HPV cannot be proven in men, which is proof in and of itself of the Illuminati conspiracy theory. In fact, back in the ancient days of fucking (10 years ago) HPV was still called genital warts. HPV aside, there are other, nagging STDs that still exist. Usually, I am a strong advocate of the "bareback rinse/ urinary extrication" after unprotected sex. This is where, immediately post-ejaculation, you run to the bathroom and scrub your junk in the sink with soap and water, pat your dead soldier down with a towel, and then force yourself to pee as hard as you can.

You may pee in the toilet or the sink. However, even this method has its flaws. Condoms are supposed to work pretty well in the prevention of STDs, but hey, is this sex or science class? You may not know that you have an STD until three to seven days after your last skank-bang. Then you may feel an odd itch, a burning sensation, or notice some discharge dripping from the leaky faucet you call your cock. This is probably gonorrhea, chlamydia, or what the Jews call non-gonococcal urethritis. These are all curable upon visiting a doctor and taking some pills.

But all these emotions arise. "That whore! Should I ask her? No, I know it was her, should I tell her? Maybe I care about her, should we discuss this?" These are all questions for later. Right now, you need to ask yourself whether you have been with anyone else since that diseased sewage grate of a gash that passed herself off as a lady. If so, you will either need to talk to these women or change your phone number. Either way works. But let's get back to the disease. If you are Jewish, you are probably a hypochondriac, which means all of this may be in your mind. Play it out for a week. You may be inventing diseases in your messed up brain. And why go to a doctor if you don't need to? That could be embarrassing, much more embarrassing than going sterile from prolonged exposure to the clap.

Now these are all best-case scenarios. You may have a zit on your ball sack, which could just be a zit or could be syphilis, which killed Al Capone. Syphilis will spread in a rash throughout your body, but again this could be in your mind and you may just be allergic to wool, or allergic to syphilis. Don't worry about AIDS anymore; that's pretty much done. Now let's get back to your leaky dick. After a month, you will know that you have an STD. Joke with your friends about it, but go see a doctor and get it dealt with. All it takes is one day of antibiotics.

Please don't drink hooch that day as it takes away some effects of the pills and you may drunkenly bang that filthy sand trap of a whore who gave you this disease originally. Don't bother talking to her about it. She has probably moved on to ruining some other poor sap's manhood. Let her go the way of the "burning yeast infection of the traveling pants."

Hopefully, one day some asshole with a Ford F-150 will marry her, fuck her with his Crocs on while Toby Keith blares from their iPod speakers, and take her on vacation to the Dominican Republic; there, while staying in some nice four-star all-inclusive, he finds out she's a whore and he beheads her and makes it look like the local drug cartel did it.

This is how it ends, because you played your cards like a gentleman.

Proper etiquette for having sex with somebody to whom you are actually attracted and for whom you may have feelings

Many people think that this is how sex is actually supposed to happen: that we are meant to meet somebody via physical attraction and then become intellectually and mentally stimulated by her personality, develop a deep trusting bond with her, and then have sex as some sort of cherry on top of the sundae. But we gentlemen know that this is rarely how real life works. We know that very often our sexual conquests are far less than conquests; most of the time they are mistakes, luck-filled events, or acts of desperation. There is not a lot of thought going into most of our banging. We see someone and think, "I can trick her for a bit," or if we're truly confident, we see a hot woman and think, "I'd like to bang her. I'll pretend I don't want to bang her for a while so that eventually I can bang her." We rarely equate sex and feelings the way that women are rumored to. Therefore, when that odd occasion pops up and you have feelings for a woman and still want to sleep with her, you must know how to proceed.

First, you must get all the pig banging out of the way with other women. These will be acts of sex that you enjoy. Do whatever you want with consensual partners and make sure that it is just sex; you can enjoy your time together after the sex as well, but it has to be quick. No sleepovers. Then, meet a woman you like. This can be a colleague, a friend of a friend, someone that you work with. But whoever this person is, you must consider your sexual attraction to her as secondary to your desire for her companionship. You will know that this is the case if you have spent time with her and really enjoy her company without having sex. You may almost feel as if having sex with her may ruin the relationship. This is a risk that you have to be willing to take. You are probably used to having sex that is very self-indulgent and focuses solely on your pleasure. You have to throw this notion out the window when you are preparing to have sex with somebody to whom you are actually attracted.

No longer can you pump away with disregard for this woman, no longer can you use her as a gagging machine because you have been so brainwashed by modern porno, and no longer can you request that she wear eyeglasses just so that you have a place to ejaculate. YOU MUST CARE FOR THIS WOMAN! Go out with her on your tenth or twelfth date and try to forget that you have been a male slut for the last 20 years of your life and that you have viewed women as lesser beings. Treat her well on this date; have a drink or two, but that's it. Remember moderation. Go back to your place and start slowly. Kiss her for a while. Think about the fact that this is what making love is supposed to be. This is not a filth-ridden sex vacation with all-inclusive prostitutes in Costa Rica - this is amiable sex. There is a new thing called foreplay. It is actually a retro notion that is very nostalgic, but it is new to you.

HAVE FOREPLAY! Let her have foreplay with you. DO NOT JUST DROP YOUR PANTS AND BEAT YOUR DICK BEHIND HER WHILE YOU STARE AT HER ASS! Kiss each other and explore one another's bodies. Let this be a magical experience. You will have sex shortly. Be soft and caring. You may hit a point in the intercourse where it is time to get faster and harder, but that time is not a minute in. You may feel like you want to tell this woman that you love her. Even if you are feeling that and she feels the same, fight the urge. Look her in the eyes. Some nasty positions may arise, but these positions are about pleasure now, not degradation. You will both achieve orgasm.

Then there is a thing called cuddling. You will both lie in bed and trace weird shapes on each other. This will be enjoyable for awhile and then will become annoying. One of you will say, "No more shapes." Lie in bed together. You may have sex again and then you will go to sleep. Oddly, you will not think about the quickest way to get this woman out of your home without anybody seeing her. The next morning you may have sex again. Then, you may go for brunch. When you finally say goodbye, you will long to see her again. You may actually feel weird. This is what normal people call "falling in love." You may settle down and have a life together. You will feel that you have been missing this for your entire life. This is what sleeping with a woman to whom you are actually attracted and for whom you have feelings is like.

It's not for everybody. But hey, you tried it.

Proper etiquette for using the word "faggot" in public

Years ago, fashionistas introduced the saying, "Grey is the new black." This went through several permutations on the color wheel, such as "navy is the new black" or "brown is the new black," and eventually was extended to areas other than fashion. "Hip" writers would provide a unique spin to their pieces by saying "40 is the new 30," "Tel Aviv is the new South Beach," and "virgins are the new sluts." Finally, Hollywood got hold of it and made a great series called Orange is the New Black. Wrong. Gay is the new black. Everywhere you look, all of the homoerotic numbers add up and prove that if you combine the struggle for equality, the need to move into impoverished areas, and the hate crimes that happen in fast food restaurants, gay is the new black. This also means that gay people are talked about behind their backs, as well as hated and admired from afar simultaneously; this equation leads to a slang word that must be thrown around by enemies and embraced by colleagues. That word is "faggot."

Most people who use the word hatefully are either closeted homosexuals or brainwashed, right-wing-Jesus-neophytes or black people describing cousins who just came out of the closet. It's a hate-filled word, and, as you will notice, it has those two stinging syllables, much like the other word we can't use - nigger. While we can tone down the "N-word" by adding the "a" ending instead of the much more controversial "er" ending, the word faggot has no cushier form of pronunciation. To use the word "faggot," we must be completely in. Balls deep, if you will. True, the Jews figured out a Yiddish spin: "fagela." But it's a copout. It's like using the word "schvartze" for black people. It's just code. It's like using pig-Latin in fourth grade: gutless. It's not head-on semantics. We must commit all the way. FAGGOT OR NOTHING!!!!

First of all, find some gay people. They're everywhere: in the arts, restaurants, adopting babies at government offices, yelling on the streets, in glory holes, leather shops, serving coffee, bringing you meals, going to prom with you (kidding, if you're already gay you can use the word "faggot" freely and do not need to know the etiquette - please see the "Coming out of the Closet" chapter if you are gay). Befriend these gay people. Let them know that you are not gay, but that you are jealous of their lifestyle. Gay people are the last renegades on the earth. They get to do what they want, when they want. They can do molly (or ecstasy), suck four cocks, and then show up to work a brunch shift the next day. They are not expected to marry, have kids, or buy homes. They can live freely. They have the option of surrounding themselves with all the trappings of mediocrity (aka the straight life), but they also can dance, drink high-end tequila, and own French bulldogs guilt-free.

Hang out with your new gay friends at the restaurant where they work. Go drinking with them. They may try to sleep with you and even offer to suck your cock once or twice. Usually, the uglier gay men will offer. DO NOT TAKE THEM UP ON THE FREE BLOWJOB OFFER! Do not even take up the hot gay men on the free blowjob offer. Remember, you're there for a word, not a lifetime of questioning yourself under God's scornful eye. Once you get the blowjob offer and turn it down, tell the other gay men that the "ugly gay man" offered you a beej (call it a beej; it's cute and high school girl-like). The other gay men will squeal with delight and exclaim, "Oh, he's such a faggot." Wait until all of them say the word. Now is your Rosa Parks moment! Order lemon drop shots for the table and then yell out in your gayest possible voice as you are about to take the shots, "To faggots!"

Everyone will drink to your cleverly masked use of the word. In essence, you have just called a table full of gay men "faggots" to their faces, and you have broken down the walls of prejudice simultaneously. You have proven that the word need not come from a place of hate. You may now use this word again in public several times when recounting this story to others and the actual "Last-Supper" table that witnessed your breakthrough. You have done more for gay men than Harvey Milk and AZT on this fine night. Drink it in and realize that your public use of the word "faggot" was not just a victory for straight men wanting to use the word, or gay men wanting to hear a loving version of a horrific word, but it was a victory for all of humanity. Well done, gentleman. You have proved that hate can be turned into love through a word. Now go home before you drink too many shots and decide to let the "ugly gay man" blow you in the men's room.

RUN! HOME! NOW!

Proper etiquette for dating a stripper

As gentlemen, we have been known to frequent gentlemen's clubs. A gentleman's club is a very nice phrase for a strip club. These are places that we, as men, can enter, and look around and figure out why it's important to strive for wealth and fame. There are very low-end strip bars that make us think about how depressing our lives and the lives of those around us are, but there are also high-end peeler bars that can inspire us to do better. We enter the club as civilian nobodies, and then we see these beautiful, damaged women approach us and we pretend that we are somebody. For 20 bucks a song, they treat us like we are modern-day deities. Then we have the thought that if we had more money and more fame, we could take two or three of these drug addicts home with us.

Strippers have a certain appeal that stems from the gaudiness in their appearance. They dress like bums outside of their work hours because they don't need any more attention. All they get at work is attention. They dress down outside of their work hours because they can't be in bikinis all day. They usually take good enough care of their skin so that under the strip club lights they can look appealing. But if you get them out of the peeler bar, you can see all of their imperfections highlighted in pock-faced glory. These girls are far too tanned, far too lasered, and far too siliconed. Botox fills their lips and their under-eye areas, and they probably have had some kind of work done to their chins. Upon further inspection and questioning, we may find that these women have had vaginal rejuvenation.

Strippers get into the game to make money, plain and simple. There are some small-town girls who need the attention and hope to bang some bench-warming professional athletes, but other than that, it's about the money. Some of these peelers may be claiming to be saving up for nursing school. These are the girls that we refer to as liars. Dating a stripper is usually something that you want to do in your 20s but it's still possible to date a stripper in your 30s and even into your early 40s. It will help if you are a celebrity once you're older; failing that, if you are in top bodybuilder shape or a coke dealer, you will have a good chance at bedding one of these girls who has a fake name and swings on a pole to Pink songs.

First, meet a stripper. You should be in a strip club or a gym to do this. The gym idea is nice, because most strippers work out, and if you can pick one of them up outside of a strip club, that means you've got mega game. If you have to pick up your stripper in a strip club, do not spend any money on her. Also, try to go in just before the night time rush happens. When you are one of very few men in the strip club, you have a better chance than you would if the Buffalo Sabres show up. Talk passionately about what you do for a living. If you do not have a cool job, you need to go get one and then come back to the strip club. Get her real name from her as soon as you can. Get her phone number. Call her up and set up a date.

For the first date, you should do something involving drinks. Try to go to her place with two or three bottles of wine. Drink the wine. You may have to meet her three or four kids at this point. Some of the baby daddies may come through at the beginning of the date to either pick up or drop off some of these kids. They will be nothing like the nice baby daddies portrayed in Tyler Perry movies or on prime-time television. They are bottom-feeding scum. Once all of the baby daddies have come and left, it is time to bang the stripper. She will be full of life, vigor, and flexibility. You will be amazed at how tanned and smooth her skin is. She will smell like a baby. This may creep you out a little bit as you will be fucking a hot woman who smells like a child. THIS DOES NOT

MAKE YOU A PEDOPHILE; IT IS MERELY HER SMELL OF CHOICE!

Use protection with this stripper, not so much out of fear of disease but rather the fact that you know she is fertile as Amish farmland and she has nothing to lose. After a few weeks, you may slip up and start banging her with no protection, but you will be smart enough to pull out. Now that you are dating, she may long for a traditional kind of life, and she may talk about getting out of the game. THIS IS JUST TALK! This woman has no education and could only fall back on a waitress job if she were lucky. You will start to know the people at her work. They will be an eclectic bunch: door staff, waitresses, other strippers. You may even be so lucky as to have a three-way with one of the other strippers. These are truly some of the best days of your life.

But soon the allure of this titty-filled nightclub will wear off. You will tire of her crying infants and the "pussy-to-stress ratio" will outweigh the benefits that you once found so appealing about this failed burlesque dancer. One day, you will accidentally pre-come inside of your stripper just prior to pulling out. She will think that she is pregnant. You will have to tell her that you love her but that you're not ready for a kid, and you will present abortion options to her (refer back to the chapter on "Proper Etiquette for Dealing with a Pregnancy Scare," in this case). She will say that she loves you, too, but will add the disclaimer that if she believed in abortion she would have done it four kids ago. YOU ARE NOW FUCKED!

You have danced along the razor's edge by dating a woman about which most men can only fantasize, but now she wants to keep your kid. Try being an asshole to her instead of taking the nice guy route. If she thinks that you'd be a dick to be around, she may decide to abort the kid, but she may also decide to have the kid out of spite to teach you a lesson. Isn't it amazing that women who spread their pussy lips for tips can take such a moral high ground on abortion and God's view on procreation? Luckily for you, you are a degenerate male and, as such, have probably contracted HPV at some point in your career. The pregnancy scare is just that: a scare.

It will turn out that she has some type of lesser-known cancer in her reproductive organs thanks to you passing HPV along to her, and that is why her period was late. She will not know that the disease came from you because she has had more white dicks in her than a lady boy Thai escort. There will be a few awkward moments, but then you will be free to go about your life. Don't call her anymore and avoid this strip club and most other peeler bars in the tri-city area. Stripping is a small game, and many girls who stripped with your fake-named princess will hear about what an asshole you were.

One day, she will see you on television and think about how lucky she was to bang you.

Proper etiquette for coming out of the closet

As a straight man who never had to come out of the closet, this may be a difficult form of etiquette for me to perfect. So allow me to paint the broad strokes, and you can fill in the rest by trial and error. Allow me to be clear: I have had homoerotic experiences, it's just that I prefer women sexually and therefore am not gay. You may have had straight experiences, but are gay. This chunk of etiquette is for you. First of all, you may not have gone to prom with your lover. If you did, there was probably a big thing about it on public access television; that would have "outed" you. You may have met George Takei on a daytime talk show. If you did, you may already consider yourself "outed". You may have gone to a Miley Cyrus concert with friends and tweeted about it; "OUTED"! Other than that, you may be living a shell of what your life could be. If you are gay and are in the closet, you are an idiot.

See, there was a time in the 60s, 70s, 80s, 90s and early 2000s when "gay" was frowned upon. You were looked at as less of a person and made fun of by others. Now, "gay" is an asset. Many companies have gay quotas to fill, and your career success is virtually unlimited if you are gay. You will skyrocket past many more qualified applicants in the job market if you are openly gay. Chelsea Handler will offer to hang out with you if you are openly gay. You will make a ton of money on MTV or any major network show if you can sing or dance. And, let's face it, if you are gay, you can probably both sing and dance. You probably sing and dance all day long in front of the mirror. You probably take good care of yourself and therefore are perfectly suited for a life on television.

Even if you are not gay, you may consider coming out of the closet merely for financial gain and career success. However, you may get found out if you become too successful. The gay civil rights fight has not been a short road, so if you lie about being gay it may ruffle some feathers in the hate crime unit. But if you are really gay, tell somebody right away. It's like being touched by a bad person when you were a kid:

"Go, run, tell someone!" This will be hard at first. Choose someone you trust: a fat friend, an ugly ex-girlfriend, or a gay work colleague. They will all want to take credit for your "homo-ness." They are self-indulgent losers. You are the fag winner here.

Now you will have to tell your parents. They will accept you however you are. They will question their parenting for a few weeks and think that either they screwed up or their drug use during pregnancy made God make you wrong. Sooner or later, they will watch the news and see someone who is gay and famous. This person will be on the news because he overdosed on drugs or alcohol. Then your parents will think, "Maybe our gay son will be famous." Then they will be happy that you are gay. Then they may think, "Maybe our gay son will overdose." Then they will be sad and they will reach out to you. They have made an effort. Now every holiday and family dinner will be awkward, but at least you can rest assured that they don't want you to overdose.

Next, you should come out to all of your bitchy ex-girlfriends. This will make them feel like it is their fault that you are gay, and they will question both their womanhood and their sexual abilities. They may even go so far as to ask if you became gay because of them. Look them in the eyes and say no, but let them know that you are lying. Next, come out at your work, and whenever shit doesn't go your way, make people know that you think it is because you are "recently gay". You can sue the fuck out of any workplace. If you are black and gay, all it takes is one major lawsuit and you can retire in the Mayan Riviera. If you are

Jewish and gay, you will get no sympathy. It's almost like the two minorities cancel each other out.

Next, run through the streets and proclaim your gayness. Take in gay culture. This includes, but is not limited to, drug use, dancing, casual sex in public places, bad theatre, threesomes with fat women, poppers, brunch, mimosas, and seeing people you used to know in your straight life who are also gay now. Buy a Smart Car, or a Mini or a Fiat or a convertible Mazda. Fuck everyone you meet, then slow down and get into a monogamous relationship after you get gonorrhea from a man's butthole.

Eventually get a French bulldog, listen to opera, vacation on a small island near Florida, and go antiquing. Get an apartment in a gay village in a major metropolitan area. Grow old. Get bad tattoos. Enjoy James Franco movies more than you should. One day, you will eventually pass away. Now aren't you glad you came out when you did? That wasn't so hard, was it?

Well done, gay gentleman.

Proper etiquette for attempting to break into the porno industry

Some things are best left to the pros, and porno is one of them. I know we all think that we possess the ability to fuck well if we had guns held to our heads. But the honest truth is that many of us are horrible fucks and don't deserve to eat up any digital space on an HDD camera. That being said, sometimes gentlemen need to try things to prove to themselves that they can't do these things. Start out by going boozing at a bar. Meet up with a friend. Get some cocaine! Cocaine is what porno people use often;

whether it's to get them over the emotional atrocities that led them to a life less ordinary, or the need to feel accepted among a group of their peers, cocaine comes in handy in the porn game.

Get some cocaine. Do the cocaine at a bar. Look at all the women you want to sleep with but know you can't get. Mention this to your friend.   Go on about how women in major metropolitan cities are wenches or lesbians and play hard to get. Now, you or your friend should bring up hookers. At first, joke about hookers and how you would never pay for sex. Then be honest and mention how many times you have actually paid money for sex (and if you've been paid for sex, this may be a good time to brag). Go back to your place and order two hookers. It is probably 3 or 4am, so you will not be getting the best hookers possible, but you will get hookers with mouths and vaginas (usually each hooker will possess both of these attributes).

If your hooker does not possess a mouth or a vagina, YOU ARE FUCKING A MOUTH-LESS MAN! STOP! Go back to getting a hooker with a mouth and a vagina and start over. Set up a video camera in your closet, and cover the red light with tape. The hookers will arrive. Do cocaine with them. Order more cocaine from people they probably know in your building. Do more cocaine. Go into your room with the hooker. Your penis will not work right away. This is not the sign of a porno star. YOU ARE A FAILURE! If you were in "the business," you would get fired on day one. You would be costing the production time and money. You would have a director yell at you, "Time is money, you flaccid-cocked Jew, get off my set." Good thing you're not on a professional set.

The hooker will be blowing you with no condom, and still, you can't get it up. On set, people would start wondering if you really even like pussy or if you're just doing this gig for the money and a shot at going to the AVN awards show to see what Vegas is all about so you can fuck dudes on the down low. The hooker deals with this regularly; you are not special. She will offer you some GHB. TAKE IT! It is the date rape drug, but as they say, you can't rape the willing. Still, no hard-on. This has been an hour of you trying to wedge your floppy excuse for a dick into her mashed-up sin bin. It's not like she's tight. This is an easy fit: your tiny mushroom tip and her gaping cum gash.

The Dave Matthews band CD, Live at the Gorge, is probably distracting you. Let her blow you a bit more, finally get hard enough that you can bang for a minute or two "doggy-style," and then fake an orgasm to end the awkwardness of what is happening here. She will leave. Turn off the camera. Why did you think you were good enough to fuck on camera? The drugs made you think it. That's why most people do porn. You failed. You are at best an amateur. So, the next time you jack off to people fucking on your computer, have respect for it and know that they are doing something you cannot. Well done, gentleman. You have learned that if you ever meet a porno star, you will not look down on him; you will look up to his bravery.

Porno stars are the true heroes after 9/11.

Proper etiquette for regaining sex drive as part of a mid-life crisis

We spent most of our late 20s and early 30s in pursuit of a dream we thought that we could achieve. We were renegades when we were younger; we wanted to tip the world back and drink from its cup of greatness. We were trailblazers. Then we made a bit of money, and gone were the days of living it up, for we got mildly content. We met pretty girls; they were good enough in bed, so we settled down. We got into serious relationships, and that led to marriage or engagement or some kind of monogamy, where even if we cheated, we would never admit to it. We forged a life together with our "soul-mates," who slowly became our "dream-killers."

Somewhere in the middle of these relationships and in between career success and financial stability, we found ourselves eating a little more, exercising a little less, and copulating less than a virgin who thinks the back door is the "only way" due to Catholicism. We began to stay up later, drink more to make the pain of either monogamy or monotony go away, and one day we woke up and we were in our late 30s. We used to love sex. Sex used to make our decisions for us. Even though we were born with dreams, vaginas were what made us chase those dreams. Vaginas fortified us to go after our desires, to make more money, to work harder, to be a success; then we got those vaginas and they tore our souls out. So now we're older, much more distinguished, and alone.

We may have fucked a lot immediately after getting out of our relationships, but now we're dried up, fat pieces of sexless shit. It's time to get it back. First of all, stop smoking, stop drinking and stop doing whatever the fuck else is dragging you down into this suicide pact that you have with government-approved stimulants or depressants. GET YOUR FAT, OLD FAILURE OF AN ASS BACK INTO THE GYM! Throw out your dick pills, because you're not gonna need them anymore . . . actually, keep a couple just in case.

Now go out and buy yourself some new clothes. Get something nice - think outside of the box. Dress like a gay man would. It's amazing how much less threatening and how much more attractive you are when you dress gay. Men look at you, women see men look at you, and women want what men want; that's how bra-burning and female executives in Hollywood got on the map.

Now that you're all dressed up, try to eat decent for a bit. Your penis will actually start to work again now that you've eliminated most of the fats from your overly Americanized supersized diet, along with the cancerous tars from cigarettes that were figuratively cluster-fucking any blood leading to your cock and the faggot juice (aka red wine) that was lowering your libido. You may even start to wake up with a hard-on again. Touch it just to prove to yourself that it's real, but don't jack it, as you have business to attend to.

Take your dressed-up ass out on the town. Don't take a wingman; you already look gay enough in your nice clothes, and you don't need to end up in a steam bath with a handlebar mustache bouncing off your lower abdomen prior to an exchange of 40 dollars. Go to a place where there are women. Target a vulnerable-looking, large woman. Wait until the black men have all cleared away from the large woman and she stops "twerking" against the remaining parasitic black men. Go up and talk to her. She will be impressed that a well-dressed white man who doesn't smell like Cool Water, Drakkar Noir, or Snoop Dogg is talking to her. Ask her name. She will tell it to you. You will forget it. Ask her where she's from, what she does, where she lives. Tell her you live nearby. Make a joke about stalking her. She will laugh, because she knows you wouldn't stalk her; if anything, she would stalk you. YOU ARE ABOVE HER! Why? Because you are somewhat successful, dressed like a fag, and have the moxie to talk to a woman who just fought off more black men than fire hoses during the Watts Riots.

Ask for her number. She will give it you. You forgot her name. GET HER NAME NOW! It will be less awkward than when you fuck her and don't know it. Don't say, "Shit, I forgot your name, if only you were more attractive." Instead, say "How do you spell your name again?" She will say, "Jen . . . you don't know how to spell Jen?" You respond with a joke like, "I didn't know if it was one 'N' or two 'N's' - you never know with you crafty white women." This will make her think that you didn't forget her name, you are witty, and you have slept with women of all colors. As a result, she will now try harder in bed to convert you back to "team white-chick." Your sex drive is back. Leave abruptly. Make sure that you booty-call her over the next week. You will come very quickly. Even if you can have sex twice in a night (which you will be able to, I believe in you), it will only be enjoyable for you. She will garner no pleasure whatsoever, other than lying with you afterwards and possibly having your penis as a placebo meal in her mouth (in my experience, large women have the best blowjob mouths because their jaws get so much practice with food).

But good sex takes practice. That's exactly what this was, practice. So what if you came before you were fully inside of her and then you pumped for a few more seconds until you went fully soft and unleashed a blood-curdling moan to make her think that her pussy was a majestic de-humanizer? You may see her once or twice more, but now your confidence will begin to boom. Much like American foreign policy during a war, you are back in the game of fucking people who had no intention of getting fucked. You may even end up friendly with "Jen with one 'N'," but now that your sex drive is back, you're ready to up your game to employed women who only take up one seat on the subway. Well done, gentleman: you made a big girl somewhat happy post-coitus and you are preparing for your future with hot, middle-aged women.

The world is your oyster, and, ironically, you no longer require oysters as aphrodisiacs.

Proper etiquette for a one-night stand with a fag hag, black girl... on her period

Inter-racial sex is hot. There's no two ways about it. It proves that we live in a post-racist world when a black girl is willing to be as promiscuous as, if not more than, a white man. First of all, you must meet a black girl. There was a time when this could only be done in places such as Harlem, Africa, inner-city ghettos, post-riot marches, and the backs of buses. But not so recently, a thing called "equal rights" came along. It is now possible to meet black women in all the same places that you could meet white women, although there is still a very high proportion of black women in Asian nail salons. Many black women will be into one-night stands because they are curious about white sexual prowess and they would never dream of taking you home to their parents, since you probably don't have a criminal record or fatherless children running around the country.

Go to a bar. Take some of your gay friends, who inevitably work as waiters or bartenders and are struggling singers, actors, dancers, or some combination of all three. Hang out with your gay friends and flirt with them. Mention sucking "cock" and ponder why God may or may not have made them wrong in the eyes of Republicans and question how their parents dealt with the disappointment that accompanied these young "artists'" lives.

This will guarantee comfort in this alpha male gay group. At this point, their girlfriends will come to the bar. Chances are, these fag-hag girls were out at another bar flirting with straight men and couldn't make it without the wing-man ability of their fine-feathered faggotty friends. The gay service staff will now chat you up to their girlfriends, because although you are not a "Liberace at large," you have pretended to understand the gay man's plight (which, by the way, in 2014 isn't as much of a plight as it is a gift).

Wait until the bar closes. Go outside and smoke. Watch as the gay men hook up and make out. This will make the women horny. They cannot reach out for the gay men's affections, so a black woman will now ask for you to make out with her. DO IT! Get in a cab with her. She will tell you that she is on her period. This will disgust you. But sometimes vaginal meat is best served rare. Get back to your place. Make sure that there are no bears or hungry dogs around. Undress her. Undress yourself.

Usually you would lay a towel down and fornicate in a Haitian blood-fest on your bed. But black women bleed more ferociously than white women (this ideology is both racist and unproven, but I bang black women on their periods, so I can't be racist). Instead, take her into the tub. Bang her doggy style. Watch as the blood collects on the condom (oh yes, wear a condom. I forgot to mention that before. If you proceeded without a condom, you may be dead now from a rare string of Rwandan AIDS). CONDOM! NOW!

Do not comment on the blood collecting, or as it pours down her legs like someone finding oil in the film Giant starring the late, great James Dean. Ejaculate. Toss the condom. She may lie down in the tub from exhaustion, disappointment, and blood loss. She will want you to hold her. Stroke her caringly, but do not lie in the tub . . . YOU PISS IN THIS TUB REGULARLY! DON'T TELL HER THAT!

Watch as the blood running down the drain reminds you of Elizabeth Shue's scene in Leaving Las Vegas; goddamn, sex with a black girl fag-hag is cinematic.

Clean up and go to bed.

The next day, chat about life and fishing and the Jim Crow laws of the South. Send her to a sketchy deli for breakfast. Above all, respect her. The next night, you may see your gay friends again. Ask them for the black girl fag-hag's phone number, and her name.

You won't call her again, but pretending you will makes your gay friends think highly of you.

Proper etiquette for sleeping with a friend of your married friends

We used to like getting set up in our earlier years. We would have friends bring us pussy served up on a silver platter. Then after years of ruining the relationships of couples or friends that set us up, we decided to go rogue into the world of sex. We wanted to be libertines and make our own way in the world. We were under the impression that our own qualities should be able to get us laid, and we felt like we didn't have to rely on colleagues or friends to bring us unsolicited gash. But as we age, we find that we are often too caught up in our own careers and ambitious pursuits to spend the right amount of time chasing tail. We are mature now, right? We can accept the fact that when help is handed to us, we need not turn it down. It's not charity if we put in the proper work to fuck our friends' friends with the dignity they deserve. Open yourself up to the universe and watch how it fulfills all of your one-eyed snake's desires.

You will want to find a married couple; they will either want to set you up so that they have another couple to do things with or so that they may destroy your solo happiness out of marital spite. There is also a third option where the married couple remembers that they don't have sex anymore. The man in this relationship will be okay with celibacy, but inevitably the woman misses sex and is of the opinion that if she's not having sex, her friends should at least be getting boned. If you are friendly with both people in the married relationship, your guy friend may resent you for getting pussy when he's not. Too bad for him; he made a choice to become a sexless statistic and now he has to live with it. He may also be worried that if you get close to the girl with whom you're being set up, you may leak stories about prostitutes or awkward three-ways that took place under a bookshelf. We all make decisions in life, and if your friend didn't want to regret his past, he shouldn't have taken on a degenerate friend like you who makes your life about the quest for enlightened debauchery.

The married woman in the couple will introduce you to a single friend who isn't getting any "cockage." She will try and set you guys up expressly for the purpose of coitus. The single girl in the set up may be okay with this, but there is a reason that she's single, and it's not because of promiscuity. It's because any time she gets a man near her pussy, she mistakes fornication for love. Women often confuse these things. As a gentleman, you know that sex and love are different and very rarely occur in harmony with each other.

Since you still want to be friends with your married friends after this whole thing dissipates, you must treat the set-up chick with respect and dignity. Call her before you intend to go out with her. Do not treat her like a diabetes-ridden slob who lunches at McDonalds; in other words, do not try a first-night booty call. Let her know that you would like to go out with her. She will happily respond in the affirmative and will move all of her other plans to the side. Her other plans probably include purchasing cat food and using a purple vibrator to stimulate her clit while watching Downton Abbey.

The first time that you go out with her, meet her and have a few drinks and make her laugh. Then walk her back to her car. Give her a couple of gentle kisses goodnight. Don't go any further than that. Now go get some rest; you will need it to reclaim her born-again virginity the next night. While you are resting, she will be texting your married friends, mentioning what a proper gentleman you are and how funny you were and how cute or sexy she thinks you are. The next time you see her, she will be thinking about fucking you. If you don't emit the vibe that you want to fuck, she will want to fuck you even more to prove she is not a spinster. Have a few drinks, make her laugh, and then she will invite you back to her place. You could take her to your place, but what's the point? Go to her place and talk her through the sex.

You probably didn't stock up on dick pills, so you too will require a little bit of coaxing into sex. Go gently and slowly. Pretend that it is the first time for both of you. This is actually exciting! Her cats may be bothering your allergies, but what is a gentleman to do? Killing her cats in front of her would turn her off, and you haven't come yet. We make sacrifices for fresh poon sometimes. The fact that you have no dick pills means you will be unable to wear condoms. But what the fuck, right?? It's almost like you know each other. You have friends in common and your friends don't have AIDS, so you should be okay thanks to deductive reasoning. But remember to wash your cock in the sink and pee after every load you dump on her trim midriff. Also, you should towel off her belly with a warm washcloth after every load you dump on her. "What a gentleman!" she will think to herself.

You will surprise yourself by being much more intimate with this woman than your average one-night stand. It will almost be romantic, the way sex feels for ladies, but don't fag out on me now - GIVE HER A FEW HARD PUMPS JUST TO REMIND YOURSELF THAT YOU ARE A DEGENERATE! Also, get her to gag on your cock a little bit without being too rough. You will amazingly go for a second round and then will pass out. You'll be tired, but drag your fat ass out of bed and wash your cock in the sink again. When you lie back down, she will tell you that she is on the pill. WHO CARES? If anybody wants you to father a child, she is on crack. There's a thing called the morning-after pill, which makes proper birth control nearly archaic.

The next morning, after a horrible sleep due to cats and mutual regret, you will wake up hard again. Go use some of her toothpaste to rid yourself of your morning breath (it probably smells like a cruise ship sommelier crapped cheap red wine poop into your gullet as you slept). Come back and give her another round. Cuddle with her a bit. Remember, this is not some dime-store syphilis-skank. You shared intimate moments, much to your chagrin. Get out of bed and have her make you some coffee. She will cherish these moments. She hasn't had a man bang her well for years. She also hasn't been able to use her capacity for nurturing since her post-secondary education began.

Allow her to make you eggs while you write. She will think that you are writing about her. YOU ARE WRITING ABOUT HER! TELL HER YOU ARE NOT WRITING ABOUT HER! Have coffee and a few smokes and pretend that you are interested in what she does for a living. Get dressed. She will drive you home after trying to fuck you for the fourth time in a 12-hour time-span. YOU ARE NOT SUPERMAN! GET THE FUCK OUT OF DODGE! Kiss her goodbye and go rest your cock.

You haven't seen that much action since you were 18, when your dick worked better than your brain. Your cock will be sore. Her pussy will be sore, but she will hope to fuck you again later that night. Try to find a polite excuse not to see her. Hopefully, neither of you gave the other a disease, and hopefully, she is not pregnant. She probably likes you, and her biological clock is ticking far too loud to justify an abortion. Within a week or two, you'll know if this set-up has any legs. If it does, your married friends will want to see both of you a lot more than often. If it doesn't, you will look like the bad guy even if the woman boils your pet rabbit.

So go on about your life; either way, you handled it like a gentleman.

Proper etiquette for when you are a white man living in Harlem and there is a late, all-black party happening in the park outside of the projects next door

Usually these parties will have blaring music, cheap cognac, and drunken people who have lost hope six years into the Obama presidency. But they still believe "Yes, we can" and party until all hours on a Wednesday night. Now don't be fooled. Some of these people have jobs, but most of them are not running off to early-morning surgery. They live in the projects because they have jobs they hate, and most of these jobs don't pay well. That is, if they have jobs at all. This is truly a socio-economic experiment. Do we blame their workforce woes on race or predetermined social factors? USUALLY RACE!

Many of these people live off of the government - hence the term "community housing." Now, bear in mind many of these folk are angry at the system and will not listen to a white "authority figure," let alone a white man with a degree in philosophy, so approach with caution. There will be many pit bulls and large black women. Do not confuse the two. The pit bulls have four legs. The large black women have one or two legs, depending on the type of diabetes they have. Ensure that your first words do not contain the words "brother" or "sister." You can't use "brotha" or "sista," either, because those are more offensive coming from a "cracker". Do not ask, "Nice party, who just got out of jail?" You will be stabbed and perhaps confused for the low-quality pork ribs and end up barbequed.

The proper etiquette for this is to merely hope that the party stops soon. There is nothing you can do. Have you not watched prison films? Black people will fuck you up if you go into their part of the yard! Perhaps they will run out of weed or Alize. You can pray that there's an outstanding warrant for one of the organizers and the cops show up to take Lionel back to Rikers. No matter what, do not tell them you are gonna call the cops. In this case, you would be branded a snitch. You may think they will not recognize you on the streets, but let's be realistic - gentrification isn't as commonplace as we'd like in some neighborhoods. They will be able to tell you apart from the other five whiteys. And if you're straight, the four gay white men in your neighborhood may help rat you out for weed favors from the local tribesmen. There are two irrefutable facts in low-income areas: gay men love weed, and black men love selling weed.

With all of this acquired knowledge, it seems like going outside to complain about this party may be counterproductive to staying alive. Therefore, the best thing to do is stay inside, look out the window, and let your anger build. Do not act on it. When you wake up the next morning, throw some used condoms into the park. If you do not have a date to help you produce used condoms, masturbate angrily into the condoms to images of Nubian princesses. When the pit bulls eat the condoms tomorrow, they will feel your anger. Even though technology has evolved so rapidly that we all hold mini-computers in our hands as telephones, this is as close to solving a loud black party as the white man has come.

The proper etiquette for doing cocaine with TV/film stars

We all have dreams in life. Many of us dreamed of being world-famous and wealthy. This dream happened for very few of us, while the rest of us grew into embittered sculptures of life's mediocrity. But there are still chances for those of us that have given up. We may think that we will never rub elbows with the modern day gods and goddesses of media stardom, but there is a way. First of all, get your foot in the door with some kind of production company. You needn't be educated or even good at your job. Just be in the right place, right time. The right time is soon; the right place is anywhere that gives tax breaks for production in North America or Prague (wherever the fuck Prague is). This includes dilapidated cities like Toronto, Winnipeg, Halifax, anywhere in North Carolina, or, once again, Prague.

Get a job as a transportation person, set decorator, or even a "Genny-op." All of these menial jobs will get you close to stars. However, you may break many codes of conduct as a lowly member of the crew, so although you may have both cocaine and access to stars, you will not look like a gentleman when you do blow with these slightly talented, highly insecure moguls of the screen. So take a year or two and learn how to act decently enough to book television roles. Then work out and grow a goatee to look tough so that your acting niche is far less competitive. Then audition until you land a job.

During this audition phase, which is full of rejection, you will meet other "actors" dealing with rejection through either drugs or yoga. Find the ones who prefer narcotics over stretching as a coping mechanism. Do coke with them. During this phase, you will meet future TV stars and you can hold their addiction over their heads in years to come when their roles as the 'token brown guys who talk white' for four seasons on a highly watched nerdy sitcom dissolve. You will also meet theatre stars and "wanna-be's." Cocaine still attracts some cool people.

It also attracts Latin people. So do cocaine discreetly, or you will have to hang out with Latin people.

Then one day you will be lucky enough to book a film role with some major stars. Make sure that you don't talk blow right away - wait till week three of the seven-week shoot so that you don't get labeled a druggie. We save that term for the stars. Hang out with one British film star coming off of a Woody Allen movie and a huge box office actor who has now hosted SNL twice and gets hotter pussy than a crematorium. Do coke with one of them. Do a lot of coke!!! Steal some of his coke when he gets up to piss. Then bang a female crew member poorly (cocaine messes up your dick, unless you are black or a liar).

You partied with movie stars, so they will tell you to call them when you go to LA. THEY ARE LIARS, THEY LIE FOR A LIVING! They are not your friends - it's just that you did coke with them and paid for half of it, even though their per diem is far larger than yours. The key to remaining a gentleman throughout all of this is not telling anybody; although it would be cool to brag about the people with whom you party, it's way cooler not to. And if you ever do tell the story, don't mention names, although IMDB can give many helpful hints.

And remember, gentleman, as an African-Canadian male stripper once told me, discretion is the greater part of virtue.

Proper etiquette for drinking and driving without getting caught by authorities

We all catch ourselves doing some things we know we aren't supposed to be doing. Drinking and driving is one of those things; if we're not careful, cops can arrest us for what seemed like a victimless crime before we killed two pedestrians racing to get to the 'international waters' of our driveway where we believe all illegal things to be legal under some kind of Geneva Convention. Then the next thing we know, we're in prison at the bottom of the anal rape food chain because although we committed manslaughter, it was vehicular at best; then we have no cred, can't walk the yard without our hands in another man's pocket, and our anal fissures have garnered us weekly visits to the medic. Well, don't fret. A DUI needn't be impending if you follow these steps.

Drink with some sort of pacing and method to your madness. You're out in the afternoon and you have a car. REMEMBER THAT YOU HAVE A CAR! This will keep you from getting black-out drunk and will keep your eye on the prize, which is to get home in one piece without a criminal record. Meet up with your friends and mention that you drove. They won't give a shit, but at least you will have witnesses that you tried to behave, and these people may turn out to be accomplices should you kill anything tonight. Have a few glasses of wine. Feel the buzz kicking in. Accept the fact that you are a man and have grown up quite well. YOU ARE DRUNK IN THE DAYTIME! You are living the life of a modern-day, North American god. You don't need a job that limits your day drinking. You are probably five glasses of wine in. Now slow down. Go to the bar and meet a woman. Flirt with her. Go have sex in a hotel! Make sure that you achieve orgasm. Coming will make you feel more sober.

Whoops, you just had sex with a girl you met at a bar and paid for a hotel. THAT HAPPENED FAST! That is a traceable offense with credit card history. If you have a wife or a girlfriend, you are screwed. You may as well drive into a pole. Otherwise, well done! You just had afternoon delight with a stranger. Now you may go out and have a few more drinks elsewhere. Try to realistically limit your blood alcohol level to one drink per hour. This is "close enough" to being legally sober that you can still tell the difference between right and wrong, even if it's just on instinct. You will need instinct to get home.

Get behind the wheel of your death machine vehicle. Have a lot of gum. Chew that gum while smoking cigarettes. This may cause oral cancer, but that is better than "dick in your ass in jail cancer." Open the windows to get the smell of your snatch-lathered testes and the moonshine-still quality of your sweat out of the car. Drive to relaxing music. Something jazzy! To avoid inspection points set up by the authorities, the key is to drive the roads that rich people would drive on. Drive the roads that lead to the good neighborhoods. Even if this takes you out of your way, remember it's not how quickly you get home, but that you get home at all. Highways are a good option, but a lot of the roads leading to highways have impaired driving programs waiting for you. So keep to the main streets, drive the speed limit, and try to look as white as possible. If you spot a visible minority, drive behind him for as long as you can. He will get pulled over before you.

In the worst-case scenario, you may get pulled over. Your heart will race when you see the flashing lights and the six or 12 police cars. DO NOT PANIC! Do not pull a U-turn; they've seen that trick before, Einstein. You also cannot drive through the trap and run over the cops as in Grand Theft Auto; these cops have other cars and they will catch you, and although killing a cop may give you more juice in prison, it still isn't the smartest choice. To quote Denzel in Training Day, "You wanna go home or you wanna go to jail?" We wanna go home. Pull up slowly to the officer. The general attitude you want to have is that this is an unwelcome delay to your otherwise sober night, but you want to layer that under the false veil of understanding and an acknowledgement that the police are keeping the streets safe for sober people like you.

ACT MOTHERFUCKER! Maintain eye contact with the officer. Only answer what they ask. Do not offer additional details. YOU HAVE HAD NOTHING TO DRINK! If you mention you had one or two drinks, they will make you blow and you will blow over. Handle yourself with brevity. Just like this:

COP: "Anything to drink tonight?"

YOU: "No."

COP: "Nothing at all?"

YOU: "Nope."

COP: "Where you coming from?"

YOU: "Work."

COP: "Where do you work?"

YOU: "The Ford Plant."

COP: "Have a good night."

YOU: "Thank you."

WOOO-HOOO. Do not yell woo-hoo. Get home and vow to never do this again. You will do it again. But always remember the gentleman's code of etiquette when driving shit-hammered.

Proper etiquette for being a functioning alcoholic

We all love a drink every now and again. We never used to. Remember when the taste of alcohol used to repulse you when you were younger? Unless, of course, you were raised in a housing project in South Boston; then you probably loved the taste of booze because it took away from the taste of blood in your mouth caused by being hit by your father while he yelled, "You ain't never gonna amount to nothing." But for most of us, alcohol was an acquired taste. We dabbled with it as teens, hit our stride when we were in our early 20s, got more connoisseur-like as we aged into our 30s, and found what we really liked. We went from sipping beers, to chugging beers, to experimenting with shots. We started with tequila until we found ourselves throwing up in swimming pools and wanting to fight our cousins, then we downgraded to B-52's, broken-down golf carts, and finally Jagermeister (before it went all fraternity).

Then we found beer bongs and drinking games like beer pong and the century club (a shot of beer every minute for 100 minutes). We learned that alcohol could erase our inhibitions and get us into sexual encounters with women outside of our usual fuck trajectory. Then we would drink on special occasions, and we got introduced to scotch. We thought that we knew how to deal with hangovers until the hard stuff found us. Back in the beer days, we would wake up, have another beer, and go for greasy breakfast. Then as we aged, we found that the hair of the dog and the hair of a Greek man's head in our eggs wouldn't act any longer as cure-alls. We had to sleep in later and let the red wine or scotch work its way out of our systems slowly. Food was required, but the eating could not just be at breakfast. We needed an all-day kind of feeding. Then we found that an afternoon nap and a masturbation session would help bring our heads back into the game. Then we found that important stuff we had to do wasn't getting done, all because of the fact that we were partying so hard on the hooch. But isn't alcohol a necessary evil in our world?

We know that we need it to network and we need it to be loose and it helps get business deals done and it helps us get rid of stress and the government taxes it, so it must be okay. Why is it okay??? BECAUSE YOU HAVE BECOME AN ALCOHOLIC!!! You have had run-ins with the law. You have almost gotten into bar brawls, even though you're way too old to be fighting (unless that fight is for control of your bowels). You are an unacknowledged friend of Bill W.

Now that you have admitted you are an alcoholic, you have several options. You can seek help; this usually requires admitting that there is a God and sitting in church basements with a ton of losers (who are way worse off than you), drinking a lot of coffee and smoking way too many cigarettes. Or you can white-knuckle it through and decide to be sober and focus on your dreams and building strong, long-lasting relationships, but what kind of fun would that be? So instead become what most people call the middle ground: a functioning alcoholic. You still get to do everything that you need and want to do and you get to drink through all of it.

First things first: make sure that most of your friends are also alcoholics. They cannot be recovering alcoholics. You may have one or two friends who are recovering alcoholics, but any more than that and you will feel like a failure. Even though you are doing more with your life than these recovering saints, you will feel like a loser by comparison. So hang out with people who still like to drink. Make drinking your top social priority. Any time you go on dates, out with friends, or even to a cultural event, make sure that booze is involved. You can pre-drink alone, but you don't want to get too wasted before meeting your colleagues. For this, beer is best. You may polish off a bottle of wine solo, but if you do, make sure that you have at least an hour to nap and half an hour to fill yourself with coffee. Keep shots to a minimum as a functional alcoholic. They can take you by storm and really throw you off your game.

In public, try to go to places where you know the bartender. This will result in your spending less money than you would at some strange place where the bartender doesn't know you. Avoid strip clubs and high-end night clubs. They may seem appealing because of the attractive pussy quotient, but these places are money traps, and even if you could get close to one of these women, you couldn't afford the upkeep on these high-maintenance hos because you have an alcohol addiction which requires most of your disposable income. You will have to learn that booze takes most of your money, so find cheap places to replenish all of your lost nutrients. Dollar pizza joints work well, and you can count tomato sauce as a vegetable, cheese as calcium, and bread as your carbohydrates. If you are truly hung over and have to go to a day job, you may begin to experiment with Pedialytes. This is an invention meant to rehydrate children who suffer from excessive diarrhea or vomiting. And what are you but a child who refuses to grow up?

Hopefully, all of your co-workers were out until 4 am with you and they won't judge you. If not, you must continue to make up excuses for your drinking.

"Special occasions" work well as does mentioning that you had company in from out of town. Continue to be a functioning alcoholic as long as you can. This will guarantee that your life is fun and filled with joy. Eventually, you will begin to wake up with regret. This is not just regret from the prior evening. It is regret that you are 40 and single and live in a glorified hovel. You may need to sober up and make amends to the 14 women you advised get abortions. Other than that, you are a great functioning alcoholic. Now decide if you want to continue chasing your dream of being the next Bukowski or learn to enjoy life without fermented grains in your body. No judgment here.

To me, either way, you are a gentleman.

Proper etiquette for dealing with your male-pattern baldness in accordance with movie-star looks

It happens to most of us. Unless we have some kind of hybrid Italian/Irish heritage whereby we were graced with the follicular genetics of our mother's father, many of us at some point go bald. Losing our hair is being emasculated by nature. It makes us feel less like men. We could have massive bank accounts, fat dicks, and beautiful wives, and still we feel like shallow vessels of manhood. We do, however, live in a society where, thanks to "possibly gay" action stars, we have many options.

We can accept our baldness like a Jason Statham. Statham has made it acceptable to be a middle-aged hero with an accountant hairdo. That being said, he is in top shape year-round. If that is a sacrifice that you are willing to make, you may be able to gracefully let your hair fall out and keep it trimmed very short. If you choose to grow out your patchy "back of head pubic look," you will be confused for a Jewish lawyer wherever you go. You could be a total party animal, but people will still mistake you for Sean Penn in Carlito's Way.

Letting your baldness embrace you will help you in some careers. If you are attempting to be an everyman commercial actor or a New York City-based improviser, the "au naturale" look goes a long way. You may also be able to find a wife, but she will run the relationship and your "guy's nights out" will likely occur at home with your wife watching via a nanny cam. Your second movie-star option is thanks to a man named Vin Diesel, who is "so straight." He is "so straight" that he has a wife or a girlfriend at the time this piece of etiquette is being written. Who would have a wife or girlfriend if he were gay? Nobody! That's who! So Vin Diesel is "super straight." Agreed, legal team? Never mind that he basically took on the "bear" look from gay subculture and made it go "straight mainstream." HE HAS A GIRLFRIEND OR WIFE! Therefore, he is straight, right? RIGHT! He shaves his skull down to the bone. This look works for muscular men.

If you are skinny, you may need to tell your friends that you either have some kind of debilitating cancer or you were imprisoned and had to join the Aryan nation for safety reasons. Otherwise, as a muscular man, the shaved look will help you break into the MMA, various bouncer jobs, or standup comedy. You could also attempt to fit into mainstream society with this look. People will always make jokes about how tough you look or how you look like you have some Latin in you. Everybody will know that if you didn't shave your head, you would be a patchy-looking motherfucker. That's why people shave their heads. You are not hiding your baldness. You are just making an aesthetic choice. The lie is known.

The third option is really not an option. It is not acceptable. But it is on the table. Get work done. Most successful movie stars who have not aged gracefully have done it. Sylvester Stallone, Nicholas Cage, and Matthew McConaughey . . . it isn't pretty, but if you can deceive yourself, as most gentlemen can, it may just work. There are two kinds of work you can have done to your dome: surgery or a wig. Some people call it a hairpiece, but it's a wig. If you are a working actor in Los Angeles, you can go for the surgical option. It will cost you roughly 10,000 dollars, and you will have to take a few months off of shooting whatever "attractive person crime series" you're working on. You will get a scar on the back of your head, and the top of your head will be a bloody mess for a while. But soon, you will have that long-desired, full head of hair. People will know that you've had work done, but hopefully you have a publicity team good enough to get older pictures of you taken down off the Internet (i.e. Jeremy Piven). Hopefully, throughout the healing process, your sham of a wife doesn't tap your head too hard while you're eating her out.

The wig option is a mistake. But we wouldn't be the gentlemen we are if we didn't make mistakes. You will go in for a meeting at the Hair Club for Men. If you are in Toronto, you can go to the location near Fairview Mall. They will scan your head with a futuristic instrument that will show you where you have lost hair. You could also do this without these assholes and this futuristic instrument using a "mirror". Then they will size your head and order you a hairpiece. You will have to grow your hair in for six weeks. This will be awkward. You will want to keep your head hidden. You are dumb enough to think that if nobody sees your head during this process, they will think that you miraculously found the fountain of youth. Buy a toque or a large selection of baseball caps. When your hair is grown in enough, you may go back to the Hair Club for Men. Ironically, there will be women in the club as well. These women are way worse off than you since they are getting hairpieces and they are women. Imagine if you were a woman who needed a hairpiece. GROSS!

Anyway, the staff will fit you for your new hairpiece. They will glue it onto the back of your head and tape it to the front of your head. You will think that it looks good. YOU ARE WRONG! Female members of the

Hair Club staff will come in and tell you it looks flawless. THEY ARE FELONIOUS HAIR CLUB WHORES! THEY WOULDN'T FUCK YOUR LYING ASS WITH A HOMELESS WOMAN'S CUNT!

Go home with all of your shampoos, combs, sprays, gels and your bill that will be charged to your VISA every month in the amount of 350 Canadian dollars. Go out on the town. You will think that people are staring at you. THEY ARE! YOU ARE WEARING A WIG! Some people will not notice your false horse head. These people are weed addicts who are only concerned with their own worlds. Do not judge your look based on the reactions of potheads. Most of them wear ponchos and think they are better than alcoholics.

Soon, you will have some hairpiece-related success. You may get a promotion or a movie role in a horror film called Bad Meat which will only ever be released on Amazon (although the film has a good director, financing falls through and you are left high and dry). You will go back to the Hair Club once every three weeks for touch-ups and new hairpieces (ironically, when you brush the hairpiece, the fake hair falls out, just like your real hair did). One day, you will look in the mirror and realize that you have less integrity than a reality TV producer. You will throw out your hairpiece, cancel your Hair Club membership, grab a set of clippers, trim your head, and then shave it bald.

You could have leased a Porsche Boxster for what you were paying monthly for a wig. You will now make jokes about your hairpiece and leave it with your ex-fiancé. She will put it in a storage locker, and it may turn up in three years on an episode of Storage Wars Canada. Clearly option 1 (bald but trim) or 2 (shaved to the bone) beats out the "getting work done" option. Or so I've read. (This chapter is entirely based on fictional characters and any resemblance to any person, living or dead, is purely coincidental).

Proper etiquette for dating a prostitute

Although we like to think of ourselves as the pinnacle of evolution, we are not. We know what we like and what we dislike, but sometimes these two worlds collide and we end up acting in a way that seems contrary to our nature. Man has instincts to lead him toward what is best for him, but on occasion our instincts lead us toward a much more interesting life choice that is not as much productive, as it is good fodder for tales of despair. These tales will come in handy around campfires or on late-night talk shows at some point much later in our lives. Living outside the box can be dangerous, thrilling, and rewarding; it can also involve dating a hooker, which is none of those things.

The average male knows the role of a prostitute. Prostitutes can come in handy during long periods of pussy drought. They can be great to celebrate the wrapping of a TV or film project in which you have starred, and they certainly prove themselves as useful during bachelor parties. However, most people never think of dating hookers. Pimps date hookers, but only during the courting phase of their business transaction. This involves the pimp banging the shit out of the young girl who just got off a Greyhound bus and is new to a city looking for fame and fortune. This banging is both a proving ground for his alpha male qualities and an exorcism of all the past family love that this woman harbored.

The pimp turns this girl out and gives her a sense of worth in letting her know that her sexual abilities are economically viable in a capitalistic marketplace just prior to taking all of her worth away and putting her out on the street to earn for him. Eventually, the hooker begins to long for her old life but knows that she cannot have it. Whether she evolves to call-girl from streetwalker is up to her, but she has been brainwashed that love is merely a four-letter word in a long list of four-letter words that have no meaning, including hope. It is your job as a degenerate gentleman to re-instill hope into this withered flower.

First, you will need to find an attractive hooker. This is not as easy as it may seem to the man who is not well-schooled in the world of sex for money. Most hookers, although they were attractive at one point in their lives, are now hideous. They are used to late-night streetlights hiding the blemishes and imperfections of their faces. If you are lucky enough to live in a city where you can find streetwalkers, drive by the track one night and look at these hideous truck-stop monsters. On occasion, two or three women will look publically acceptable. Choose one of these. These are the higher-end escorts and have some semblance of esteem because they have been used by movie stars that have been in town. Sheen, Estevez, and maybe even Lou Diamond Phillips have banged these women while on benders, and that makes these prostitutes think that they are better than they are.

If you choose, however, to date a call-girl, you will need to have many show up at your residence before you find one that likes you enough to allow you to date her. If you are fortunate enough to date both kinds of hookers, the call-girls are more intimate as they may be working for a service instead of a pimp. They still feel as if they have some love to give. In both cases, you will need to be completely jacked and ripped to date a hooker. They are used to fucking over-the hill "schlubs," and when they see your glistening temple of a body, they will wonder, first, why you are paying for sex, and, second, why you are single.

Inquisitiveness is the doorway to opportunity. If you have already banged the hooker and paid for sex, you will now be in a position where the hooker wants to see you for free. If she is an incredibly successful hooker, she may even begin to pay you for fucking her just to see what role-reversal is like. But this is not dating; this is merely a business transaction that reaffirms what a good fuck you are and how degenerate of a gentleman you can be. Instead, for the purposes of this exercise, I would recommend that you date a street-walker without having sex with her. This is a much more fulfilling social experiment and requires oodles of etiquette on your part.

Approach an attractive streetwalker. She will tell you that her name is Diamond or another gemstone. Make small talk with her. Ask her how work is. Make sure she sees how ripped and jacked you are. She may think that you're a cop. After visiting her for the fifth or sixth time over a period of a month and never propositioning her for sex, she will no longer think that you are a cop. Get her number. She will still think that you want sex. She is stupid. YOU WANT TO DATE HER, NOT FUCK HER; WHAT A STUPID PROSTITUTE! Also, remember that you should never pay for this girl's time. You are better than the horny house-husbands who pay to enter this woman's hell-hole in the back of a family minivan.

She has probably given you a number for a burner phone that she keeps away from her pimp. She will text message rather than call you back, and if she does call you back, it will be from a payphone so that Mandingo, her pimp, cannot trace her history. If he finds out about you, he will beat Diamond bloody. Take Diamond for walks along the pier and to parks. She will eventually relay her past and the experiences that led her to being a hooker, which is still a step above being a ticket scalper. Ticket scalpers are lower than human traffickers - it is a fact.

On your third or fourth date, you will make out. Do not let it go past this point. You have kissed a hooker; try as they may, most men can never accomplish this without paying an extra 500 dollars. You have defeated the system; you have caused a professional sex worker to become intimate with you. You remember Pretty Woman with Julia Roberts? This is not easy work. Eventually, Mandingo will find out that Diamond is out walking through parks with you when she should be earning, and he will beat her senseless using her burner phone that he found under the mattress: ironic, no?

He may call you and threaten you. Change your number and avoid downtown for a while. If you bump into Mandingo at a reggae party one night, just play dumb. After all, you got into this game to date a hooker, not to fight a pimp. What does he take you for? The opposite of a gentleman, that's what.

You do not fight pimps. You are a gentleman.

Proper etiquette for saving face while prematurely ejaculating

It happens to the best of us. Throughout our sexual careers, we will be "newbies," "studs in training," or "fuck monsters," and then as we enter our 30s and 40s we encounter the normalcy and stagnation of monogamy. In the world of monogamy, poor sexual prowess is acceptable since we are often the economic providers for our female counterparts. Sex takes a backseat to comfort. However, once we are smart enough to divorce or end the engagement to our women, we will be faced with going back into the cold, cruel world of dating. Our fuck quotient goes down as we become older and less attractive and our bodies become battered and bruised from years of rejection in a harsh world.

Fucking, like anything else, requires practice. Masturbating can help build up stamina in our minds, but it does little in the way of real-world experience. The actual feel of a real vagina is a shock to the penile membranes in comparison to our calloused appendages known as hands. When ending a drought as a youthful fornicator, one could masturbate prior to the date and then have some kind of longevity during intercourse. However, as age takes its toll on sex drive and erectile dysfunction, masturbating prior to sex may guarantee marshmallow cock, which is both a sense of embarrassment and a reputation wrecker among the social media of "slutdom."

Do not masturbate prior to sex; merely insert and think about something disgusting, such as Rwandan slavery, maggots in a pussy, or Tom Hanks' face at the end of Philadelphia. Failing this, if you come prematurely, continue pumping for as long as you can until the woman realizes that you have gone soft. This means that if you are fucking as you should (without a condom, or, as the French call it, "sans condom"), you will come inside of your partner. Merely pull out, look your woman in the eyes (this will be the last time you do this), and say, "This isn't right; we should stay friends." She will believe you until she stands up and your man poison drips down her legs. Too little, too late: she is already on the way to the subway. Good save, gentleman!! Now go wash your cock in the sink and don't skimp on the soap.

Proper etiquette for dealing with a cock-block from a supposed friend

We have all heard the line "bros before hos." This is a mantra set up by some closeted gay man who clearly works in an MTV office and uses the mass media to spread his own reason for justifying his homo-erotic "straight" relationships. This line makes him feel as if it is actually okay to put women and their sexual and intellectual prowess on the back burner in order to help your fat friend move a couch. He is wrong. "Bros before hos" is wrong. It is "wronger" than human trafficking, it is "wronger" than Syrian death camps, it is "wronger" than the Holocaust, it is "wronger" than remakes of nearly perfect original films, it is "wronger" than using the word "wronger."

But in this V.P. of programming's mind, 'bros before hos' makes sense. It lets him go on motorcycle trips to San Francisco with his best friend that he met three weeks ago on Grinder instead of pleasing his wife, because, hey, she's a ho and his bro is a bro. So thanks to TV shows and Hangover movies, we now think that it's ok to hang with just the guys instead of chasing the carrot that is fresh pussy. First, you must put yourself in a situation in which you can be cock-blocked; this in itself can be work. Meet a woman, preferably an Australian actress. Get her number. Intend to go out with her a few times, but always have it fall through. Then take her to a baseball game or any kind of organized sporting event. Have fun with her. Tailgate, eat hot dogs, and drink beer. Then invite her to see you in your element later that night.

First go home and shower and nap off the beers and let her get better smelling - for Christ's sake, you've been in the hot sun drinking beer and eating hot dogs all day, give her some space. GIRLS NEED TO SHIT TOO! Then meet her. Let her watch you be wanted and artistic at the same time. Will Ferrell did this very well with Christina Applegate in Anchorman, in which he played jazz flute. This is what you want to do. Set up a place where you are well known and then show off your artistic side, unless your artistic side is interpretive dance, in which case you may wish to re-evaluate your entire life and may wish to take a gay job at MTV and get on Grinder. Let her see you rip shit up. Now finish with that and go to the bar. Indulge her stories about fine Australian wines and how she was a sommelier when she was a struggling actress (which means she probably still is a sommelier since you've never heard of her nor seen her in anything). Eat things with truffles on them.

Soon, you may bump into a friend who is a struggling artist. He has never envied you, but you are working game in New York City and are out with an attractive, exotic woman. He looks like Woody Allen in middle school. He may be a little jealous, which is why he brings up the story of how you once pimped a Persian girl. Quickly take note of this and remember never to help him again. YET BE POLITE! Mention how he is at the bottom of the game and how he strives to have a career like yours built on integrity and truth. Then briefly mention the pimp story and how it was prescient of you to live through that kind of self-loathing, as it became a great story later and you have since realized that the sex trade is a horrible thing. Make up a lie that you now donate your time and money to women's liberation charities and you very often perform for the troops who have been ex-prostitutes in Okinawa.

She will not know that this is made up, as Australian people are more worried about what hostel they're staying in that night than any falsified world events. She may not believe your lie, but ply her with more wine and she may. Now is the time to lose the loser. Tell them you have to go next door. Bring her, lose him. It is always hos before bros. He will text you later and mention how great she is. Do not respond to him. You now have an uphill battle in removing this woman's panties. She either is more turned on than ever before because she knows that you are a true alpha male, or she despises you because she knows you ruined a girl's life. Feel out the situation and don't force it. Get her in a cab. This will make her want you regardless of whether or not she thinks you are scum. She may even feel excitement about living her dream of becoming a pimped-out house girl. Have sex with her or wait until next time.

Either way, you handled yourself as a true gentleman and now have room for a new friend in your life, since that weasel of a "bro" is gone.

Proper etiquette for dating a girl who used to be a slut

Sluts appeal to men; that's how they became sluts in the first place. They have a manly quality insofar as they get along well enough with their male counterparts to sleep with a lot of them. They don't have the awkwardness of an actual "lady." They feel no shame, and they love sex. They are the way that many of us want to spend our Saturday nights. But much like trees in the wild forest, sluts too must grow up. If we have been the male version of sluts ourselves, aka "worldly scholars," we may feel guilt for our past transgressions against the vaginas of the world. We may feel less like men when in reality we are more manly by passing our seed into condoms and IUD' d uteruses across the world. In feeling less than perfect, we may seek out partners who have also committed regretful actions throughout their lives.

Welcome to the ex-slut girlfriend phase. Sometimes you choose to marry this woman as well as just date her, but take one step at a time, gentlemen. Sluts are attracted to other sluts. Your new slut girlfriend won't be hard to find. Look in bars, comedy clubs, baseball games, subway cars, free health clinics; reformed "freebie whores" are everywhere. They are not limited to major metropolitan areas, either. Ex-sluts are very well known in smaller cities and farm towns as well. All one has to do to find a small town slut is "request around" or look for bathroom graffiti. In fact, online services can also help locate "once-were whores." Merely look for the single mom online who says she loves her kids more than anything; she doesn't. I'LL TELL YOU WHAT SHE LOVES MORE THAN ANYTHING: COCKS AND FAILED MARRIAGES! So finding the woman of your low-self-esteem dreams won't be a problem. What you do next will be the problem, as you still need to court a "slut of yesteryear." Here's where the challenges begin.

Other men will see you out with your ex-brothel employee and will recognize her from somewhere - usually from her having been naked underneath him. Some of these people will be your friends, acquaintances, and colleagues. We are all grown-ups here. There is no need to feel as if you are taking somebody's sloppy seconds, because in reality you are taking a lot of somebody's sloppy 250ths. Now fear not. Merely ask the ex-chlamydia carrier about him, and she will say that they dated during a rough time in her life and that he was probably an asshole. BUT YOU ARE WITH HER NOW!

On your first date, you may bump into five or 10 men that she used to bang, but remember, you used to bang all willy-nilly too. Take her home and fuck her poorly. Don't try to fuck her poorly, try to fuck her well, but it will be impossible because you have the image of her getting railed by a junior varsity football team. Try to get it up and do your best. Clearly, she's not in this for the sex. Her pussy has been beaten by more black men than Reginald Denny during the L. A. riots. She is now ready to settle down with you.

The plus side to dating a slut is that you can freely reveal your old "sexcapades" in front of her. Tell her about all of your old three-ways, banging African American women on the rag, getting HPV - all the stuff you can tell your buddies. In fact, it's as if your new girlfriend is one of your buddies, except that her labia are still swollen from a vacation to Costa Rica 12 years ago and she would blow Derek Jeter for a baseball signed by a farm team player. She is fun to hang out with, at home. But every time you go out in public, you meet another one of your colleagues, whom you thought nobody would ever fuck, who clearly sprayed his paint all over your girlfriend's vaginal walls like a young graffiti artist in the Bronx looking to make his bones. NOW, MAN UP!!!!

This was in her past, and you have to learn to accept that. I've dated women who told me they had been date raped, women who had been raped by their Jamaican brothers, and women who admitted to parental incest. These women had no choice. You can stay with these women because they were victims, not whores of choosing; if you are enough of a man to stay with an ex-whore, good for you. But if you're like me, you'll ride it out for a year or two, max, and then convince yourself that you're better than you think you are. You deserve a girl who has spent a little bit of time in the trenches, but you don't want the female equivalent of a grizzled army vet who went back to Nam because he liked the smell of chopped-up Charlie in swamp water.

An experienced woman is one thing. A woman who has had more black in her than the American prison system is another. Bang her for a bit, and then move on. When your friends ask what you were thinking by staying with her, mention that you actually liked her. She was a cool chick. They'll agree. Then move on with your life, get more successful, and stop banging women who were petri dishes through their 20s and 30s.

Proper etiquette for receiving a blow job in a cab

Some cities are unfriendly to the cab blowjob. These are usually cities with hipster cab drivers: Portland, Seattle and Boston. However, cab drivers in New York City, due to its high population of immigrants and gay men and its condescending dash of liberalism, will not stop you from getting a blowjob in their taxis. If anyone stops you from sexual expression in NYC, it may seem homophobic. Even though the blowjob may be hetero, the act of sucking dick is still gay in NYC. (Please note: I am not a legal expert, nor a noted gay advocate.) That being said, first you will need a girl to perform a blowjob. Get someone from a good family who is enrolled in theatre school. These girls are young enough and spoiled enough to want to make a mistake in public. Their sense of entitlement, combined with their daddy issues, makes them want to act out with older men.

Get drunk with this girl. But don't get too drunk (the implications toward the latter part of the blowjob may be drastic). Once you are drunk, hail a cab to go back to her place. You ideally want to be at least 50 blocks away from her place, as the blowjob requires some setup. Get in the cab. You will be tempted to make out with the girl right away. Fight that urge. Instead, talk to your cab driver; take an interest in him. Ultimately, your cabbie is the conduit to the oral sex soon to take place. Ask him which area of Bangladesh he is from. If he is not from Bangladesh, quickly backpedal and correct yourself with Pakistan, India, or Haiti. One of these is correct. Ask him how he felt leaving his surgeon job and his family back home. Ask him where in Sunnyside, Queens he lives now and how much he loves America. This will take a moment or two. Be patient. You need time to bond with Kunal, or whatever his name is. All systems go.

Now make out with the drunken girl, who, no doubt, is impressed with your ability to fraternize with the plebes of society. Put her hand on your junk. She will sheepishly begin to suck you off. Continue a slight conversation with the cabbie. Do not let his accent turn you on. You now have two options:

(1) You may come in the girl's mouth if it feels okay. If you select this option, you may now drop the girl at her place and have a good chuckle with the cabbie as he drives you home. Please tip him well.

(2) As an older man, you may not come from oral alone. Get out of the cab with your mid-life crisis erection, tip the cabbie with the 20 bucks you "borrowed" from the woman, go inside, fornicate and either leave after copulation or stay for morning sex and a diner breakfast (her treat, of course).

Now cross "cab blowjob" off of your etiquette bucket list.

Proper etiquette for dealing with a woman who thinks that she is way hotter than she is because she lives in a neighborhood densely populated with Dominican immigrants

Dominican people are great at a couple of things. Having a lower per capita rate of AIDS than the people who live on the other side of their island is their first miraculous feat. Think about it: mere feet away from an imaginary line on some Caribbean island, there is a strain of AIDS that hit Haitians with a thunderous strike from God's stealthy forearm, and then over in the Dominican Republic, way less AIDS. Any mention of Haiti brings up an image of a population plagued by HIV/full-blown AIDS, but mention of the Dominican Republic evokes thoughts of socks and sandals. Here is the second thing Dominicans are great at: baseball. No real reason, but look it up, it's a real thing. That is pretty much all that Dominicans are great at. I know some people may mention cuisine, culture, and music, but bear in mind that I said "great," not decent enough to be mentioned in a Dominican pride flyer.

Oh, I forgot that Dominicans are great at making troll-like women feel like princesses. They can take a three and make her feel like a 10, even though in their Dominican minds she may be a seven. Here is why this Dominican cat-calling has the effect that it does: desperation. A girl usually lives in a Dominican area in North America because although her parents may have money, she wants to prove that she can make it on her own in a major cosmopolitan city. She moves to a Dominican area because rent is cheaper. Due to the cheaper rent, she has disposable income to burn on fast food, cheap beer, and morning-after pills. All of these low-cost items, although great impulse buys, tend to wreak havoc with the female torso after a little bit. So she goes from a size two to a size eight as quickly as a date-rape-filled semester at Iowa State flies by.

Now, these girls are great for us gentleman because they're fun to bang, they come from money, and they can make you feel better as a person after you've gone through a break-up. However, beware - DOMINICANS

MAY BE SCOUTING OUT YOUR WHITE WOMAN! They may be having parties in minivans outside of their apartment buildings, sitting in folding chairs, listening to the same song over and over with incredibly loud subwoofers, but if there should ever be an evening when you treat your chubby love muffin with less respect than her father believes that she deserves, the Dominicans will smell this on her like she is a fried smelt and they have just returned from a hard day of stealing tools from their workplace. They will make her feel good. They will yell out things and call her "angel" and a "white beauty" - these are all things that you don't need in her brain. It may cause her to think that she can do better than you; this will result in her expecting you to pay for meals, listen to her, and visit her anti-Semitic, Aryan nation family somewhere in Western Canada. THIS DOMINICAN ATTENTION MUST BE CURBED!

Before you can solve this, we need to take a step back and bring this bloated beauty back to the one percent side of things. Dress up nice, but tell her to dress casual. Take her to the whitest area you can think of. Usually, these areas have condos that are owned by Asian people. Take her to dinner and feed her from the trough she calls a restaurant menu. Let her see how much attention you get because you are dressed far more nicely than she is and you look as if you are doing her a favor by taking her out. Let the gay waiters shower you with affection. Accept it as you begin to feel better and better about yourself and she begins to realize that the only reason she has been getting all of that attention is because she lives in a neighborhood where the two greatest feats of these pussy-hungry thieves are not being geographically disposed to imminent AIDS and waving a wooden stick at a baseball.

She must feel so good being near you. Now, let her go back to her life as an unpaid extra in the real-life version of the musical In the Heights. You have regained your confidence and can now date closer to your playing field. Or maybe you can go bang it out with a 23-year-old waitress. Well done, gentleman. There was no overt cruelty on your behalf, you brought a woman back into the real world, and now you're back on your feet. Please note that if the woman lives in a heavily Jamaican area, you should avoid her at all costs. She will have a false sense of bravado and probably has her hair braided into cornrows.

Leave her be.

Proper etiquette for crossing the border when you have something to hide

As modern-day degenerates, we have learned the pleasure of flight. We are glad that our ancestors suffered to find a way to get us across continents in mere hours. We are ungrateful that so many comedians have found the minutiae of flight so intriguing. But we are grateful for planes. We are very grateful for first class, although we can't always afford it, and we are smart enough to know that it's not worth the upgrade on short-haul flights, although first class will get you next to the awkwardness that is

Joan Rivers as she goes between La Guardia and Toronto in between Home Shopping Channel appearances. So, it may be worth the upgrade fee just for the story at times. The gift of flight is truly a blessing and helps accomplish many things quickly.

We used to be able to travel with Ziploc bags of weed in shampoo bottles and take steroids in Tylenol bottles over international borders, but since 9/11, we have been at the mercy of all the conspiracy-theorists-turned-freedom-fighters, turned border-patrol officers. Although for the wealthier, regular traveler who has gone through an intense background check, there are now several programs aimed at speeding up the otherwise arduous task of crossing a border, such as Nexus and GOES, there are still problems crossing the border for many.

Here are the best ways to prepare for flight-related issues, if you are driving across a border, it should only be to drive to L. A. for pilot season or to shop in Buffalo. In that case, ensure that you have your car detailed before traveling so that all of the pot seeds are vacuumed away, and then you should have nothing to worry about.

Now for air travel, try to be white. White people usually have the easiest time crossing any border. White people usually have the easiest time when it has to do with any kind of authority figure. If you are not white, there are several surgeries that you can undertake to lighten your skin tone; however, these surgeries are very time-consuming and expensive. Another option if you are not white is to act as white as possible when at the border. Lose your ghetto slang unless you are a very recognizable sports or entertainment celebrity. SPEAK AS WHITE AS YOU CAN! You can learn this white vernacular from BET comedians; however, this would mean that you would have to watch BET for five minutes; just guess at the accent instead. Talk how your white friends talk - not the white friends you actually like, but the white friends that you ridicule.

The best way to prepare for a flight is to get drunk the night before. This ensures that you will get some sleep. Otherwise, you will lie awake waiting for the alarm clock to ring. Drinking also ensures that you will be tired the next day, and this will cause you to yawn often at the airport. Most regular travelers are tired and focused on getting to their destinations; the yawning makes you look like a regular traveler with nothing to hide. By having something to hide, I mean crossing a border to work with no work papers or an early arrest that is on your record. If you are traveling with cocaine or a big drug shipment, this chapter will not help you. Instead, you need to find wealthy friends with cartel ties who can charter you a plane. I have no experience in this field.

When you finally get to the customs officer, approach with a big yawn. Have all of your paperwork ready to go. If you have a hat, take it off as both a show of false respect and so that the loser can see that you look like your passport photo. Avoid using your cell phone and have it turned to vibrate. You don't want NWA's "Fuck the Police" ringtone blaring when you're being grilled by a failed cop. Only answer the questions that the officer asks. Do not volunteer any additional information. If you are crossing the border for work and don't have the necessary visa, tell the authorities that you are going to visit family. The scent of booze on your breath will lead the officer to believe that you are an ordinary Joe and hate your family, which is why you were up most of the night drinking. You have now bonded with the pig behind the desk.

If you work in entertainment and are not recognizable, do not admit to working in entertainment; tell them that you are a waiter or a freelance journalist who writes about photography. If you have an arrest record and you believe that it isn't on file, don't mention it. If you have a small criminal record for which you have been pardoned, only admit to it when asked. If the high-school dropout with a nametag behind the desk tries to make small talk, indulge him. Do not get overly dirty; these people are sensitive, and most of them are Jesus freaks. Wait for the moment that your passport gets stamped, and even then don't cry out in glee. Keep your thoughts to yourself. Finally, cross the border.

Go have a drink in the lounge.

The proper etiquette for pimping a girl who "looks 18"

Living off the avails of prostitution has always been frowned upon, to put it simply. Although prostitution has been considered the oldest profession in the world, pimping seems much more parasite-like than professional. We're not here to argue semantics. What we are here to do is teach you how to pimp quickly and effectively, garner the overall experience, and then get out of the game. We are not striving for the pinnacles of "pimpdom." We don't need to be featured in a Hughes brothers' documentary. We want to do it once to know we can do it and then go back to a sense of normalcy.

First of all, get into great shape. This may take steroids and diet. Second, learn how to strip or at least put yourself into situations wherein you can be naked in front of large groups of horny women. Now that you are a sexual god (this may take a few months), find a mentor who has pimped before. He will instill in you the proper values of a pimp. First of all, any woman who wants to be with you has to pay for your time because you are a god among men. Even if you aren't a modern-day Zeus and have insecurity issues, you must make her believe this god among men stuff. Have sex with this woman. Make sure she enjoys it. This gets harder to do as you are older, which is why most pimps start young and not in their 40s.

Now, tell her that although she looks 18, she won't always look 18. Convince her that she has to take advantage of her youth and get paid. Tell her school is for fools and she needs to move out of her parent's home. Then tell her that you are going to support her. THIS IS A BALD-FACED LIE! She is going to support you: this is equal rights in action.

Take her to a low-end strip club. Keep her bags in your car. Make her work. She will make money even though she sucks at stripping because men like a girl who tries. While she works, go party frivolously, as you now have a gravy train in this exploited woman. Check her into a 40-dollar motel. Leave her there as you go home to your parent's basement. Make sure she doesn't know your real name.

Check in with her every few days to collect money and fuck her on occasion. Now get her to sign a lease for a condo for you and her to live in. You will never move in because you have made enough money off her "ho-ing" that you now have your own nice place and a spoiler and five-star rims for your Acura. Soon she will find out you don't love her and have been using her and your real name is not Brandon Rosenberg.

You will feel guilty. THIS IS OKAY! All of the actions you have recently committed were horribly selfish, narcissistic, and full of hell's fury. Accept your guilt. You are a horrible person, but that doesn't mean that you can't be a gentleman. Change your numbers, move to another state or province, and finish a philosophy degree. Never contact her again. You may bump into her four years later at some kind of open-mic comedy show and feel as if you have seen a ghost. That is because you ruined a young woman's life.

Have no fear of reparations from the Persian mafia. She will eventually go on to become a Canadian porn starlet. So she may be happy now. Amazing how something that looked like such a self-indulgent act actually helped this woman find a dream as a starlet. Good work, young gentleman.

Also, all the money mentioned above was tax-free.

Proper etiquette for being a "kept" man

Role reversal is not just reserved for sex acts in marriage and evenings out at dated swinger clubs. It is a very useful tool in proving that as men we are capable of taking on some of the positions usually reserved for women in this bipartisan society in which we mutually co-exist. Just as women are now capable of taking on several patriarchal roles during this technological apocalypse we call "modern life," men are now able to proudly take on the subservient positions that were once reserved solely for unemployed women in the Sixties. We can now embrace the glass ceiling and proudly let our male-pattern baldness graze the seemingly limiting structure that women have fought so hard to overcome.

Being "kept" will provide you with the security and the freedom to follow your creative dreams, to a degree. You will not be able to truly spread your wings and fly into the economic stratosphere, but if you are going through a period of creative gestation, then being a "kept" man is for you. It's a great time to write a book, a screenplay, some spec scripts, your memoirs, a one-man show, or a full-length musical; take some classes; learn MMA fighting; get back in top shape; recover from a penile implant . . . whatever you need time to do, being "kept" will provide you this opportunity without all of the messiness of having a job.

Having a job may sound cool on paper. Jobs give you money, get you out of the house, help you meet people and give you a true sense of purpose. WHO NEEDS THAT SHIT??? You are striving to make art here, not increase your commercial and societal gains. Hell, if you look deep enough, you'll see that jobs have been the downfall of modern man. CAPITALISM, LOOK IT UP! Good, so you've agreed to become a "kept" man for a while. Here's how you do it.

First of all, you must be in good shape in order to catch an independent woman who is going through a time in her life where she feels strong enough that she can actually own a man. She has to have that slave-master mentality. For her to be this strong as a woman, she has had to put up with some shit in her life, and if she has put up with some shit in her life, she has certainly dealt with a lot of men; after all, men are the primary source of shit in women's lives.

She has dealt with powerful men, rich men, handsome men, well-hung men . . . you may be none of those things, yet you can appear as a liar's combination of some of those things. You want to be attractive but not attractive enough to steal focus from her; you want to pretend you have money even though you don't; you need to be well hung enough to get the job done, but not well hung enough to ruin her walk to the coffee machine the next day at work. So get in great shape. Practice moderation in the world of booze and drugs and food. Control all of your appetites. Make sure that you have a clean bill of health (no STDs; the rest doesn't matter).

Now it's time to find a woman. It's not easy to find wealthy, single women with a penchant for owning men. Go to a higher-end saloon/bar, look on those weird millionaire websites, or network among your friends who work in show business. If you are an attractive young actor who has had some modicum of success and then fell off the map because of substance abuse issues, you may still remember some older producer chicks who had a thing for you. Reach out to them and let them know that you've cleaned up. Once you find your "Momma Warbucks," it's time to take her out on a date. Go all out. Borrow money if you have to. Only the best will do. This is not to cater to her tastes; rather, it is to prove that you are a catch and that you have immaculate taste and can be a nice piece of arm candy.

Dress well for your date; order only the best wines, food, and aperitifs; and when the bill comes, reach for it. You may have to pay tonight and you may not. Either way, this will be the last time that you pay for anything. Go home. Do not sleep with her tonight. For date number two, offer to cook her dinner at her house. Make a very humble meal comprised of canned foods and cheap wine that you have brought over from your home or stolen from a nearby soup kitchen. While cooking and eating, explain that you are broke but you wanted to treat her like a princess last time. Tell her about your dream of writing whatever derivative bullshit it is you want to write or taking whatever classes you want to take. She may offer to loan you money. Turn her down cold. You are too proud to do this. Now go and consummate the relationship.

Consummate it well. Bang like this is your last free bang on earth. Make sure she climaxes in a ratio of three times to your one. This orgasm ratio is essential. Within a week or two, you will move in. She will probably have you on her credit card account within the month. She will be out for work most days, giving you time to work out, write, act, and whatever other weird shit you dreamed of doing in your middle-class, privileged upbringing. You needn't worry about money anymore. But you must always keep the house clean, keep her favorite groceries readily available, and keep the sex coming at regular intervals for her. Sex is the key to her power: whenever she wants it, she gets it. Be ready at all times. Take penis pills if you need to, but never disappoint her. You are little more than a hired white-trash gigolo, so do your job.

Plan vacations for your lady. Extravagant vacations. After all, you're not paying for them. At first, you may feel tempted to go out and bang other women; DO NOT! This is a good thing you've got, so don't you dare fuck it up. However, if it is your keeper's fantasy to be with a strange woman and yourself in the same bed, who are you to stand in the way of a dream? Being a kept man is great.

After a year or so, you may have finished your dream project, and she may even help you sell it or get it made. Once you've got the big bucks rolling in, it will be impossible to stay with this slave runner. You are now free; you have been emancipated!!! Do not look back in anger, but always be thankful for what this woman gave you. In being a "kept" man, you learned about the plight of women and may have found a life-long friend. If nothing else, she helped you live your dream and may at some point come to your wedding, when and if you ever find true love elsewhere.

Let's all thank women for supporting us gentlemen.

Proper etiquette for rough sex

The complaints about our generation can be heard far and wide. These gripes don't come from print media, or petitions or rallies anymore; we live in a world where the Internet trolls can bitch about the very medium through their message. Marshall McLuhan would have blown his brains out on chat roulette via Ustream if he were a technological innovator in 2014. We have changed all of our behaviors due to the immediacy of the Internet. Our attention spans have recessed, our immediate desires can be granted in the click of a mouse, and our debauchery is now dictated to us.

We used to be as sick as our secrets, but now our secrets are being monitored by the NSA. There are no subcultures anymore. Subculture has become mainstream, and the mainstream is constantly evolving. Porn used to be a dirty thing that we could purchase in glossy magazines or by going into the back rooms of video stores located in the cheapest rental unit of a strip mall. Now, it's all available from the comfort of our own ass-scented couches. There are two unfair things about the porno of today:

(1) the very business of porn is being destroyed due to how available and how free porn videos are;

(2) women now have access to porn just as easily as men do. The shame has been removed from porn.

We don't care that the producers and increasingly less-than-stellar "actresses" are making less and less money and that their bottom line is affected by illegal downloads. We do care that women now have the ability to choose the way that they want to be fucked. They have seen all of the plus-sized dicks and all of the "picked up in a van" scenarios and all of the Bukkake fantasies that they can imagine. This in itself is not good for the average male who fucks decently, at best. But there is now a trend that all women from "tweeny-bopper" to busty MILFS have picked up on and want to experience: rough sex.

These women watch as their onscreen fantasized counterparts are choked, slapped, and forced to choke on dick until a saliva/vomit-based liquid comes out of their gaping talk-holes. And as gentlemen, we are expected to take part in our women's fantasies. No longer do women want the soft, slow hugging, leading to kissing, leading to tender lovemaking of yesteryear followed by a couple minutes of intense doggy style and an embarrassing ejaculation on the sheets to finish. Today's modern, independent women want to be manhandled, tossed to and fro into eight or 12 different positions, forced to suck their juices off of our dicks at regular intervals, have thumbs and tongues rammed up their shit-lockers and then be sprayed with no less than a liter of our man-jizz all over their faces or their glasses.

Believe it or not, there is a proper etiquette to rough sex which must be followed. None of us want to end up in prison having what we did to our women done to us by a non-descript cellmate. There is always the fear that rough sex can end in a rape charge, or, even worse, the choke-out death of a female lover. And then where are we left? With the moral dilemma of hiding the body or turning ourselves in and saying that this woman asked to be choked?? Let's not face these horrific options. Instead, follow the proper etiquette to slapping your loved one around.

Most women who are into rough sex like to think that they have daddy issues, but they are truly all just bandwagon jumpers at this point due to the Internet. First, find a girl who is into rough sex. This won't be hard, since 97 percent of women think they like rough sex. If you get one of the other three percent, you will know that she is not into rough sex when you say,

"Look at that dirty little pussy of yours!" She will look at you like you just raped a third-world child. Merely say, "I'm kidding," and have boring soft sex. But if you've got a "real" woman who lets the Internet inform her choices, start undressing each other.

You will want to get the dirty talk in right away. Make it about her at first. Mention how great her tits look. Call them tits, not boobs or breasts. You are a rough guy. Act rough, even with your vocabulary. Once you are undressed, continue making out in a very sloppy fashion. Force her down to your cock, but don't let her suck it right away. Ask her if she wants to suck your cock. Then have her say that she wants to suck your cock. SHE WILL SAY THIS! Slap it around her face first. Hit her eyes, her chin, and finally her lips. Let her blow you. Fuck her face. Feed your manhood into her voice-box! Be an active participant in the blowjob process. Do not lie down. Ensure that you are standing. Tell her to spit on it. This is her rough sex fantasy. Grab her hair and tousle it. Not too rough at first. We want to save most of the good hair-pulling for doggy style. Then pull her up and bend her over the couch. Eat her pussy. Spit on her pussy. The motive for spitting on her pussy is feigned disgust. TONGUE HER ASS A BIT! It will taste like Jagermeister mixed with pussy. That is how ass tastes; it is normal. Then slide your dick into her as she is bent over the couch.

Condoms are not necessary for rough sex (although you may live to regret this choice). Bang her doggy for a while. Get balls deep as soon as possible. Then go into old school missionary. Attempt some mild choking as you rest most of your body weight on your choking hand. Then sit on the couch. Let her ride you. Then switch to reverse cowgirl. You will slip out a few times during this position. Don't worry, even the pros slip out during reverse cowgirl. Play with her tits while she faces away from you. The dirty talk must become a dialogue by this point. Have a lot of "you like that cock?" and she should respond with "yes, baby, give me that cock," and you can counter with "that pussy is so wet and tight." Hopefully, you have a big enough cock that she will comment on its size.

Next, go back to old-school missionary. Have her suck you off in between all of the position changes. Then, take the risk of putting a pillow on the floor for her head and get over the top of her for some pile-driver position. This will hurt her neck and it will be hard to get as deep as you can, but it's worth it in the long run. Attempt some stronger choking at this point. You will really need to be flexible to choke in pile-driver. She should love it and it will distract her from the head-on-the-floor neck pain. If you are strong enough and she is not a fat pig, pick her up and bang her against the wall. Then have her suck you off some more. Then go into your finishing move. Pound that pussy doggy style while talking shit to her. Pretend that you are a boxer and she is your number-one contender.

Finally, you are about to come. Let her know that. This may be minute three or minute 35, depending on your sexual prowess. Have her kneel in front of you while you beat your dick like a runaway slave you just caught on horseback miles from your plantation. She will tell you to come all over her (she means her face). DO IT! Once you finish, collapse on the couch. She will look confused and half blind. That look is the result of you spraying ball juice in her eyes. After you have regained your normal heart rate, get up and get her a warm towel to wipe your babies off her face. See how gentlemanly you are. You may want to go again. Otherwise, make some small talk and get her number. This girl is a champ and a good girl to have in a gentleman's stable.

GO CLEAN YOUR PENIS IN THE SINK!

Proper etiquette to staying friends with an ex that you actually cared about

Much like expired milk, we usually wait until relationships are long past their due date of being sour before we toss them. And as men, we tend to not want to end things, so we start to act like utter, complete assholes and wait for our lady to drop us. Then we feel better about the breakup. We are aware of not wanting to hurt the woman in our lives by dropping her, but we are unaware that women are far less happy trying to make something work than trying something new. In the future, if you are dealing with a relationship and you want it to end, end it. STOP FUCKING AROUND! You're a grown man, for Jesus' sake. But that's the future. Let's deal with the past.

We all have had breakups that were stinging, and we've tried to figure out ways around said breakups. We drink, smoke, bang fresh gash, drink more, throw ourselves into our work, bang gross gash, drink more, smoke more, move cities, change schools and workplaces, and maybe even try to fuck her friends. None of these things work. As we mature, we find that the only cure for most ills is time. Time cures the ability to have drinks and drive a car, time cures STDs (with medication), and time helps us topple the mountain of hurt that is a breakup. First, you must find somebody that you actually care about.

This is hard; many of us are affected by looks and think we're in love, when in reality we are just with women who make us feel better about ourselves on a purely superficial level. You don't really care about this woman; you think you do because every time you picture somebody else banging her, you get upset. This is not love. This is jealousy and insecurity that is actually brought on by her surplus of confidence. You have, in essence, become the woman in this relationship. Get out.

But one day you will meet a woman who you find so beautiful and who makes you laugh and listens to you and gives you all the answers when you feel as if you live in a world that is only full of questions. This woman will be your princess. You must treat her like a queen. You will have great sex with her, although it may not be the best you have ever had. This will make you think, "If she were truly my soul-mate, wouldn't the oral be better?" GET YOUR MIND OUT OF THE GUTTER; SEX ISN'T EVERYTHING!

You will know that you truly care about this woman not when every thing is going swimmingly but when she gets sick or things aren't looking up for her family members. You will be at her side throughout all of her painful ordeals. You will be her rock. If anything is off with her, you will be moved so much out of concern that you may weep or tears may well up in your eyes. This isn't gay - this is love. But fuck it, sometimes love is a little gay, so maybe you are a little gay, too. You will love coming home after being away and seeing her. You will hug her, love sleeping with her, and just love being with her. This isn't weird - it's called caring. This will go on for years sometimes. Then there may be a day when it doesn't feel the same anymore. You may be moving in different directions. You know it will be time to end this soon. Do it carefully. Be a man, but do not be afraid to show some emotion. Kiss her, hug her, and tell her that you will always love her. Mean it. Don't say it if you don't mean it. Move away. Help her get into a nice apartment. She does not need to go out on the streets like earlier girls you dated but didn't care about. She was your queen, so treat her that way still. Just as you became a rock for her, so too was she a rock for you. Make sure she has somewhere nice to live with convenient amenities. Talk a bit after you separate. Not too much. Fight off the urge to say, "I miss you."

After a few months, you won't talk. You will still have the baggage from this relationship. You may start to follow each other on social networking sights after a year, possibly a year and a half. She will probably be dating a cop by this time; it won't last, as cops are scumbags who trade morality for hooker hand-jobs. You will be dating a waitress or an actress or a woman who does both simultaneously with a little more emphasis on the waitress section of her life. The sex will be good and the relationship will be fun, but you are not ready to commit. Be honest with the waitress/actress. Tell her that you have baggage. This amazes new women, that you can be so vulnerable and honest. She will be intrigued and will push harder to be with you. This relationship will help pass the next year.

After that year and this new relationship ending simultaneously in a poor fashion, you will have the perspective to talk to your "ex that you actually cared about" (the one you didn't have to go see in a horrific off-off Broadway Strindberg play that didn't get any better even with half-off drinks at her restaurant). Now the "ex you cared about" has moved on after taking time to actually heal after your breakup. She is healthy and in a good place and dating a younger guy with a full head of hair and a pickup truck. You can start talking again about things you used to do together. Talk occasionally. If you had a pet together, call to check in and say hi to the pet. You may even actually go over and see the pet. The pet will be happy to see you.

Let a few more months pass. Get successful at whatever you do. Let this success ring through the television waves (a modern-day equivalent of mountains and valleys through which the message used to be spread in a tribal fashion). Drop in and see "the ex you cared about" at her workplace; her old friends may even pretend to be happy to see you. You have now realized that you can be friends with an ex. This is amazing. YOU ARE SO MATURE AND WISE! In a few months, you can even call her and tell her three-way sex horror stories about you and a hippie with a bearded artist friend of yours.

You can laugh together and make fun of people and celebrate each other's successes. It was time and action that brought this back to civility. You never know - "the ex you cared about" may go on to meet someone who may be great for you in the future, and she may hook you up with the "new girl you care about more than the ex you cared about, but it's all thanks to the ex you cared about." Think of your ex-girlfriend as a Yelp review for your very being.

Dealing with an "ex you care about" is not an easy thing, but it's a sign of a true gentleman.

Proper etiquette for spending a night in jail

For some of us, this happens earlier in life, while for others it happens later in life, but if you are truly living life, it'll happen at some point. There are many reasons why a man goes to jail or prison: he may drunkenly run over a child after an attempt to cover up his mediocre life with alcohol and a jaunt in a high-performance German automobile, he may kill his wife in a fit of adulterous rage, he may be down on his luck and get caught up in a human trafficking ring wherein the strippers are also smuggling cocaine or heroin in their snatches, or he may merely be driving without insurance. Most of the aforementioned infractions would lead to serious jail time, even with the proper team of Jewish lawyers at your disposal.

Prison is very different from jail and there are different kinds of prison as well. So don't immediately think that this chapter is all about the best way to lube up a biker cock or two with cocoa butter and insert it into your man pussy in exchange for honey buns. That is a skill you will need in a maximum-security penitentiary. Not all people get raped in maximum-security penitentiaries, but let's face facts: if you're reading a book and you don't have a bunch of Nazi tattoos covering your bruised Aryan face, you're getting fucked like you were a confused female tourist in Central Park after dark in the 70s.

Maximum-security prison does not infer that you will have the maximum security allotted to you as an individual. Rather it means that you have maximum security put on your cubicle-shaped domicile to ensure you don't escape from the daily rape, back into the world that you took for granted that had freedom and way less dick in your ass. And let's face facts: the dick is bad, but picture the sweaty stench coming off of these barely shaved Neanderthals as they fuck your face like its Jodie Foster's unwilling pussy on a pinball machine.

Of course, there are also white-collar prisons where they send politicians; there, the worst people you have to worry about are the Portuguese men who were illegally importing lobsters for their lobster and pigeon-themed restaurant. But unless you're stinking rich, cross white-collar prison off of your bucket list. Then, of course, there are short-term holding cells and little jails. You can land your ass in one of these if you are going through a mid-life crisis, so pay heed. You may have a few extra drinks on the way home to see the devil-whore you married one night and get pulled over. If you are truly intoxicated, they may throw you in a holding cell for the night on top of taking your driver's license and car from you. Or, you may get angry at a neighbor who just won't shut the music off and take a swing at him or her (equal rights) and spend a night in the pokey. Or, you may rebel against society after a particularly bad day at work and decide to snag a chocolate bar from the 7/11. Any of these little acts of defiance will end with you getting thrown into jail or a holding cell for at least a night.

Now, since most of us are grown-ups and have access to credit cards, we can usually bail ourselves out, even if our "disappointment of a wife" won't come to get us. Problem is, sometimes you can't get bailed out until morning if you get arrested later in the evening. So here's how to handle your arrest and prison time. When you get arrested, I know that you want to call the cops "pigs," "whores," "cunts," "high-school failures," or even "glorified walking pieces of dry cum in blue uniforms." Hold your tongue. These guys have the power to pass word on to the jail about how you behave. YOU NEVER GET A SECOND CHANCE TO MAKE A FIRST IMPRESSION! Be polite. Know you did something wrong, but get in the back of the car and keep your mouth shut. This will be harder to do if you're hammered. But try!

Also, don't talk about the alleged crime at all. Begin performing isometric exercises in the back of the cop car. Do this subtly. Basically, you want to flex your muscles so that when you get inside the jail you have a good pump going. This will make you look scarier. If you are not at all scary looking, do not get a pump, as this will make you look gayer and like more of a "come-receptacle" than a bad ass. The cops will take you to jail. You will get checked in. Fight the urge to ask for an upgrade to first class or a suite. These guys have no respect for satire. Cops and jail workers have their own sense of humor, but most of it involves cheating on their wives with hookers and getting blown by gay inmates for cartons of chocolate milk. Leave the comedy to these losers tonight.

The jail staff will take all of your possessions. Depending upon your behavior up to this point and how busy the jail is (this usually depends on how close low-income housing is located to where you reside), you may get your own cell. Even if you do get your own cell, do not relax yet; other people may come in throughout the night, and they will be drunker and have less to lose than you. If you do not get your own cell, prepare to act. Walk in and stay silent. What must be going through your head constantly (inner monologue) is "Why the hell did I do that? Why would I kill a man?" Even if you only stole a chocolate bar, this is the message you want to put out to other inmates.

You will see other people in your cell. They, too, have done bad things, things worse than stealing a KitKat bar. Keep your mouth shut. Even if somebody asks you a question, answer with a grunt. If they ask why you didn't answer them, grunt again. If they are white, say, "No habla inglesa" in a gravelly voice. This will throw them off and may make them think that you are part of a street gang like MS-13. They will leave you alone. However, do not do this if there are real Latin people in the cell. Prison, much like America, believes in a system built upon racial segregation, but if you lie and get caught, you are dead.

Now, it may go through your mind to fight somebody to prove your manhood. DO NOT! You will be out of here in a few hours if you keep your cool. Avoid eye contact; people will mistake your sense of bonding for a bitch that wants to make love. Keep your head down and keep silently repeating your mantra, "Why the hell did I do that? Why would I kill a man?" More people will enter the cell throughout the night. But now you have been there longer. You are a veteran of this cell. You are an O.G. for all these fresh fish now. Just hold your ground. Don't talk; keep using the Spanish card. Finally, a Spanish man will enter. Let's face it, they commit crimes quite often. You will have to drop the Spanish lie. You will be found out.

You will now have to get into an argument with the original asshole who attempted to provoke you, who will say, "I thought you didn't speak English." You may now say in your most urban voice, "Oh, that was a couple of hours ago, I done picked it up!" Stare at him. He may back down or he may come at you. If you can fight, stay quiet. If you can't fight, yell as you fight. This will bring the guards and they will break it up. Now you may get warned, separated, or transported to a real prison. Hopefully, it's one of the first two. If it is the latter, this book is no longer effective for your needs. Trade this book for some smokes, figure out how to make a shiv and a pussy out of a yogurt cup, and join a gang. Otherwise, you have made your bones. If you won the fight, you should be incident-free for the rest of the night. If you lost the fight, people may whisper "bitch" until morning breaks. Be polite to all the staff the next morning, especially the judge, as you may need to see him again.

Either way, when you get out the next morning (thank God you are white), take whatever money you have and get the best lawyers money can buy. Go to rehab, domestic dispute classes, even church. You do not want to go back inside. Lesson learned. "The unexamined life is not worth living," said Aristotle. True, but now that we've had a taste of how the cappuccino races live, we can go back to being gentlemen.

Proper etiquette for talking shit about a woman whom you actually find attractive while knowing that she is not empirically hot

Every once in a while, we go through phases in which new and exciting women enter our lives. These women can be gifted in certain ways; they may have the gift of intellect which allows us to have meaningful conversations for hours. They may be fans of our favorite sports teams and take us to several games. They may be in a business that fascinates us and allows us to meet new and exciting people. Finally, they may be incredible at cooking, sex, caring, nurturing, and essentially "knowing us" on a deeper level than we have ever experienced. None of the aforementioned great qualities had to do with physical appearance. I'm fine with that, but are you?

You've dated many women who weren't Calvin Klein-esque women, and you were never ashamed of them. You took them out and showed them off like you were a "Make a Wish" volunteer. You never judge women on their appearance; you judge them on what's on the inside because usually if you play your cards right, it's you inside of these women at the end of the night and then on a regular basis (BOOM). You are not shallow. But you understand that looks rule this world.

Looks are the reason many people on television have careers even though they possess little or no talent. These people are not merely place-fillers either, as many of them go on to achieve fame and fortune. All you have to do is look at MTV or the Twilight franchises or any vampire-related, commercially feasible programming to see that looks run the world. Times Square isn't known for its glamorous neon imagery of Paul Giamatti. Looks make everything seem better, and that's why you can't blame deodorants, toothpastes, or hair products for ruining the world. You have to exist in this post-graduate high school vacuum, so do your best.

You may care deeply about the woman who loves you, but you may be ashamed to take her out in public. You must strike first in this case. First of all, if you had real friends you wouldn't have to do this, but you probably are upwardly mobile and deal with douches you call friends. You have to disparage your lady friend first to make sure that these douches don't get hold of this info and use it to bring you down. Also, remember most of your "friends" probably haven't gotten any pussy since their last date rape in college. You need to attack your girl behind her back and all of the wordings have to come from a place of love.

None of this is misogynist or hateful, although it may seem that way at times. Make sure all of your "friends" are around as you begin this long line of digs. All digs must be smart, irreverent, topical, edgy, and not safe for work (NSFW). MAKE SURE NOBODY IS RECORDING THIS CONVERSATION, YOU INSECURE SHITHEAD WHO DOESN'T KNOW HAPPINESS WHEN HAPPINESS COMES AROUND! Keep your barbs to weight, eating habits, promiscuity, and vaginal stench. These are the lowest of insults, which means that the socially autistic "friends" you run with will understand them. Start with an insecure zinger like "I hooked up with this bigger girl, bigger than a manatee." Now start ripping:

"She's actually healthy. For breakfast, she has a pancake and a banana. I mean 18 pancakes and a tree of bananas dipped in chocolate."

"In third-world countries they call this girl the walking dead, because she looks like she would try to eat all of the survivors."

"I think I'm the first white guy she's fucked. She's had more black on her than the back of a bus in Alabama in the 60s."

"I'm not worried about getting her pregnant because I know that she would eat the fetus in the third trimester."

"Her pussy is so stagnant, it should have steam coming out of it, and a sewer grate on top of it, and a homeless man sleeping on that sewer grate for warmth."

"This girl's pussy smells so bad, it makes my eyes water when she texts me pussy pics."

"Her period blood hemorrhages so badly it could have been used by FEMA to stop the damage from Katrina when the levee broke."

"Her vagina reek is so intense and powerful that the US military is using it to gas innocent civilians in Syria."

"This slob's ex-boyfriend was so gay that Freddie Mercury called him a faggot while he came in his mouth through a glory hole in a leather bar."

"My chick's ex-boyfriend is so gay that in terms of AIDS, he is patient zero."

"I left her at home alone. I'm hoping she didn't get confused and eat the fridge."

Your "friends" are probably laughing hysterically. Now go look yourself in the mirror and realize what an asshole you are. You have something great, but because it's not publically acceptable in your circle of capitalist monkeys, you degraded your feelings for what could be a great woman. Go home and treat your woman like a princess, because at the end of the day, actions are more important than words. Of course, this etiquette advice is only for a gentleman in training. Once you have achieved true "gentleman status," you will know that you protect your woman's honor infinitely. However, there is an amendment to this etiquette lesson: if this woman cheats on you before you ever say anything bad about her, you may publicly tear her apart as part of the gentlemen's code.

Proper etiquette for smoking cigars

Smoking has been proven to kill us. Cigarette smokers run the gamut from bingo hall fatties to up-and-coming hipsters. Cigarettes are a speedy rush of nicotine and make your hand smell like you've been finger banging a tracheotomy hole. Cigarettes are disgusting. But as degenerate gentlemen, we need to smoke something. Weed is an occasional fun time, but not something that you want to get addicted to. Pot may seem cool, yet eventually it affects your lifestyle too much and makes you far too lackadaisical to be an effective degenerate. Accoutrements of success are necessary to be a modern man. This is why we dress well, we avoid minivans, and we only drink imported beer.

Cigars hit a steady comeback in the 90s thanks to movie stars and Wall Street douches. Now cigars are an affordable option for maintaining the sense that we are better than 99 percent of the population. You can't just jump into cigar smoking with no knowledge. That being said, you don't need to be a connoisseur to act like a connoisseur. First of all, find a place to buy your cigars. Avoid going to corner stores; otherwise, you will end up with "backwoods" or "swisher sweets." Leave these cigars for wanna-be gangsters who empty out the tobacco and use the wraps to roll blunts before they go on their weekly drive-bys. Remember, we are attempting to elevate ourselves from the pack, not regress to inner-city savagery.

Every major city has cigar stores. Find one of these and go in to the store. The people who work in cigar stores are huge douches, even bigger douches than the people that shop in cigar stores. When you walk in, the retail douche will look you up and down and judge you. Wear a hat that covers most of your face so that you may be mistaken as some kind of creative juggernaut who is trying not to be recognized. Ask to go into the humidor. Asshole-face will follow you in because he thinks that you're going to steal all of their prized, high-end cigars. As a white man who is relatively successful and going into a cigar store, you will be watched like a recently escaped convict. NOW

YOU KNOW WHAT IT IS LIKE FOR A BLACK PERSON IN AMERICA TO SHOP ANYWHERE!

The dime-store douche will ask if he can help you. Tell him you're just "gonna see what pops." To him, you have now feigned cigar knowledge. In reality, you are buying yourself time so that you can look at prices. That's all that really matters. You will see expensive cigars. Avoid these. These high-end cigars are way cheaper to buy online. The store puts a huge markup on their cigars because they think that we are all idiots and they have to pay rent and all that inconsequential shit that shouldn't concern us. Their overhead is fucking with our lives. Pick out a few moderately priced cigars. Pay for them. Ask for wooden matches. The cunt-faced weasel behind the register may try to charge you for matches. Remind him that you just spent 60 bucks on cigars. Get into a verbal altercation with him so that the final result is you getting your wooden matches for free. Vow to never come back to this douche-hole. You will go back on this vow. Have him cut your cigar and feel like this douche is now your slave.

Walk outside and light your cigar. Walk with your cigar. Get a coffee with your cigar. Enjoy how great life is as you smoke the succulent, big, brown cock that is in your mouth. People will think that you may be covering up a gay fetish when you smoke cigars. These people are all derivative of an early 90s George Carlin joke. They can't even think for themselves. How the hell do they know what the good life is like? THEY DON'T! Watch as people get offended by the smell of your luscious mouth cancer stick. FUCK

THEM! They offend us in different ways: their insignificant lives, their meaningless conversations, their ugly babies that are polluting the world. Smoke where you want. This is a free country, and if these fascist bastards can't take a little cigar smoke, they can leave. Fuck them and their gluten-free lives.

Traditional etiquette tells you to smoke a cigar until there is roughly one eighth remaining. FUCK THAT ETIQUETTE! We are renegades. Smoke it until you can't smoke it anymore. It will become harsh toward the end. Remember you paid for that harshness, so enjoy the whole bittersweet experience. You may become light-headed throughout the cigar, but soldier through!!! You are classy. Go home with the rest of your cigars and put them in your humidor. If you don't have a humidor, you are a hillbilly. Don't put cigars in the refrigerator. This is an amateur move and is reserved for your autistic friends who go to all-inclusive Cuban resorts and bring you back counterfeit Cohibas, wait a month to give them to you, and tell you that they should be good because they had them in the refrigerator.

Next time somebody does this, slap them in the mouth and use the dry, counterfeit cigars they brought to stop the bleeding under their nasal cavity. You may become more comfortable smoking cigars in your apartment. Your neighbors will complain indirectly. They won't have the balls to say anything to your face. Why would they? You're a bad-ass, unpredictable mother fucker with a cigar habit. They may cough and give you screw-face in the hallway. FUCK THESE LOSERS! If they knew anything, they would smoke cigars. The smell of cigars is grand. Women with daddy issues will be attracted to you more than ever because you smell like their grandparents. Drink in your new success. Watch Scarface.

You are now a gentleman with a cigar habit.

You are better than other people.

Proper etiquette to dating a waitress

Waitresses are the best. Allow me to restate that: waitresses are . . . there. They are always there. No matter where you go in this fine world of ours, as much as technology evolves, the waitress will always be there, unless computers truly take over the world and we just start getting our food out of machines. Weirder things have happened. But for now, waitresses are here and accounted for. They can look sexy in their Applebee's gear or their Hooters t-shirt which may heighten the appearance of their herpes-stained lips against a man-cave backdrop in any North American city. Waitresses are always there. It is in their very nature to serve, which is part of what makes them sexy to us. We can also sense their desperation, their unhappiness, their desire to be doing something in the arts.

There they are; those unhappy servers who think that they'll be able to get out of the game even though they're already 40. These are the "lifers." Their tits are sagging a bit, their blowjobs didn't get them where they wanted to be in life, and now they have to close tonight and open tomorrow morning. Damn you, capitalism; you crushed this wanna-be dancer/singer/actress/comedienne/writer/stuntwoman. And now here she is, all alone and bringing you German beer by the bottle.

Hitting on a waitress isn't as easy as a degenerate gentleman would think. She gets hit on all the time. Your initial approach would be to go against instinct and not talk to her about work. That is the right approach. Talk to her about the dreams that she never accomplished. Don't even mention her job. She knows that she has a job as a result of crushed hope: you don't need to remind her of this. Talk to her about what she really wanted to do with her life; this will get you out of her place of work and to a bar that she usually attends to drown her sorrows. She will know a lot of people there and you will be the odd man out. She knows a lot of people here because waitresses go there and drink and bang their co-workers or strangers. TONIGHT YOU WILL BE THE

STRANGER THAT SHE BANGS! You will go home to the waitress' apartment. You will notice lots of inspiring things that have had no effect on the waitress: pictures of her family, a live/love/laugh sign somewhere, lots of candles, and things about how important dreams are.

The waitress will probably have at least one cat. She will think that cats are better than men, but her cat probably doesn't bang her like you are about to. She will have a great deal of candles, and the bathroom will either contain a picture of New York or L. A. The waitress will have either HPV or herpes or both. Wear a condom if you can. After you bang on the first night, the fun is just beginning. Get her number. You will see her again. If you do stay over the first night, she will have to get up early and go work brunch. Leave with her, as you don't want to stay in this post-modern Wiccan den any longer than you have to. The place is probably well-located, as most waitresses who live outside of L. A. can't afford cars. She needs to be a 12-dollar cab ride from work, so there is probably stuff to do around her place.

Go home and shower her bumpy stank off your nuts. The waitress will text you throughout her shift about how hung over she is and how much fun she had. She will be sexually extraverted and will want to see you again ASAP. Put it off for a day and go out with her again. By going out with her again, I mean go fuck her again. It'll be fun. This can go on for a while. She may be into offering up threesomes with her bisexual girlfriends. Take advantage of this offer. The only real advantages to dating a waitress are half-priced appetizers and the odd free drink. The sex will be good, but you must always keep your guard up against the HPV and herpes. Soon, she will fall in love with you. IT IS NOT BECAUSE YOU ARE SPECIAL! It is because she is needy as fuck.

You will be able to stay over at her place when she is at work. It'll be comfortable. However, should you ever leave your computer or anything you wrote at her place, she will look through your emails and your written memoirs; SHE IS A PSYCHO! She will use anything she finds in your inbox as a reason to argue. The sex will not be good enough to stay with this woman who still believes she was born to make it as a movie star with no acting experience at the age of 36. SHE LIVES IN A WORLD OF DELUSION! All she is truly good at in terms of being dramatic is calling you and crying after she has listed off the soup of the day for the 28th time that shift. You need to find a way out of this thing. You can simply move cities, change your number and hope for the best, or be direct with her, tell her that she is a nut and you never want to see her again. She will appreciate the honesty, but this will make her fall harder for you. Have breakup sex and then go to the doctor and make sure that you don't have herpes on your mouth.

Also, don't go back to that restaurant for at least two years.

Proper etiquette for getting paid for sex

This will usually happen less and less as you age. But when you are young and full of vigor and your cock works on demand, you may be one of the few men to benefit from the insatiable desire for intercourse and a female's need to feel more financially independent than men. Women who have been burned before tend to use their scorn to pay back men in their lives that have pissed them off. So if a woman was cheated on, she wants to pay her man back ten-fold. If her husband was an innocent lawyer who banged his secretary, his scorned wife will bang two of his friends, four random black men, one Spanish gardener who works on the premises, and hopefully someone young for money. If you are over 35 years of age and are not a James Bond lifestyle kind of guy or an underwear model, or know some real low-life motherfuckers, it will be next to impossible to get paid for sex. If you haven't gotten paid to have sex at this point in your life, chances are pretty good that you missed your window of opportunity.

There is still one opportunity for you to get paid for sex, and that opportunity is taking advantage of the elderly. This is usually frowned upon in society and is currently termed "elder abuse." However, if you can live with yourself, here is what you do: find an elderly woman who may be a widow and offer to bang her for some of her husband's pension and part of whatever he willed his wife. You will get money for sex and perhaps even an old watch that was probably in Vietnam or another American war against some undeserving country. In addition, you will get a certain table in hell that is reserved for the rape of grandmothers, YOU SICK FUCK! Now for those of you who are much more "normal" degenerates, here is how you can get paid for sex.

The easiest way is to be young and Catholic and take part in the activities at your church. You will probably only be paid in wine, and the sex will be with other men known as "priests." Avoid this unless you want to have a life of trouble and believe in a strange, unforgiving God whose messengers play with your asshole. Odd options aside, if you are serious about getting paid for sex by women, you must be in your late teens/early twenties. Get a blue collar job that women find sexy. Be a gas station attendant, a contractor, a gardener, or a male stripper. You should be in good shape to do any of these jobs. Women may fuck you if you're a fat slob, but that will be because of your eccentricities, and they will rarely pay for those. Get ripped. You can also run an online ad wherein you offer sensual massage. However, many men will respond to these ads, and you may have to fuck a man. DO NOT FUCK A MAN!

The best way to meet a woman is in person. When you meet the woman, be confident and sexy. Compliment her on something that does not make her feel beautiful. Compliment her taste, her car, her home, or her clothing, but do not compliment her beauty. This would take all of your power away. She will ask you to "get together sometime." This is where shit gets awkward and you have to maintain your confidence. Suck it up and say something to the effect of "I'd love to but because of my job I have to charge a flat fee whenever I leave the premises, but I'd love to." Then shut up. Ninety-nine times out of a hundred, this woman will look disgusted and walk away. Sometimes she may weep. One percent of the time, she will respond with "HOW MUCH?" This is America and we are striving for that one percent. You're in. Set a price. I can't tell you what to charge, but I'd say to bang this woman for an hour, "all in" including cunnilingus and the risk of getting caught by her Russian mobster husband, 300 bucks is a good start.

Get the money as soon as you meet up with her. She may say that she has to stop at a bank machine. Let her. You don't want to risk giving away your services and then getting jack shit. YOU ARE NOT A NORMAL MAN! Tonight, you are a gigolo, a man who loves for money. YOU SELL LOVE, MOTHER FUCKER! Once you have your money, pleasure the fuck outta this bitch. She paid. Do shit to her that her husband won't. Eat her ass, spank her, cum all over her. Well done. You are truly an experienced lover. She may have had so much fun that now she wants to take you away for weekends and buy you material items. You are a hero to this MILF. But never allow yourself to be degraded from gigolo to boy toy. You must still get paid every time you bang or whenever your time is requested by this lady, even if you don't bang. Time is money for you. If she wants to take you away for a weekend, that is a weekend that you are away from your other clients. Even if you do not have other clients, you must pretend that you do in order to keep yourself in demand.

Soon you will have saved up a lot of money and will feel as if you don't need your other sexy blue-collar job. You will quit that job thinking that you can live off your gigolo/stud-for-hire, tax-free dollars. YOU ARE WRONG! This woman will get bored with you as soon as you have too much time for her. Now you are nothing but a used-up man-whore lacking adequate semen: this will affect your relationships for many years to come. Even if you verbally keep this a secret, people will read it in your soulless eyes. Try to move on. A Jungian analyst may help, but in the end nothing will heal the fact that you sold yourself. Try to avoid hard drugs and let time heal most of the wounds.

Assimilate yourself back into society, and one day try to impart the wisdom on how to get paid for sex to other gentleman. You lived a very rare life. You got paid for sex by a woman. Not as cool as it seems, is it? That's why more women are prostitutes than men; it's not just because that's what's getting exported from Russia. It's a game about the lack of morality, and women deal with it better than we do.

That is why the word "gentlewoman" does not exist.

The proper etiquette for experimenting with anabolic steroids in your 30s or 40s

Let's face facts. The body as a temple is a young man's game, as is good sex, flexibility, and an opportunity to become a star in the sports world. However, science has been able to keep baseball players hitting homers over the fence until they get suspended and then get to appeal their suspensions. It also keeps football players' bodies intact until their early 20s and lets pro-wrestlers pursue acting careers until they find out that "anti-aging science" doesn't help with acting. Science is a good thing. It may have negative side effects like premature baldness, elongated foreheads, and pissing off organized religion, but science can put an older man back in the game.

You've probably noticed that as you get older, you've picked up some shitty habits: booze, smoking, gateway drugs, financing possessions, debt and even monogamy. Even though you strive for your youth by hitting the gym, or running, or yoga, or swimming, or some other gay sport, your body doesn't react the way that it used to. That's because your nuts are older and produce less testosterone. You have old balls that want you to sit around and keep them warm; these testes don't want you hitting the gym. YOU'RE OLD AS SHIT! You may have your frame, but it's time to get jacked again, and creatine monohydrate and protein powder can only take you so far. GET IN IT TO WIN IT!

First of all, talk to the muscle-head in your gym. If there is more than one, approach the white guy (if you approach a black guy, he may think that you are a cop, or, even worse, he may be a cop with some reparation-related aggression he wants to unleash). Mention to the muscle-head how great he looks, using words like "shredded" and "diced," as these let him know that you are into the bodybuilding culture, or at least were before you were old as shit. Mention how you used to bench 315 but an injury slowed you down and now you're looking to get back into the game. Have conversations with this tiny-cocked, shriveled-sack, lunkhead for a week or two. Talk about his bouncer/account executive lifestyle and befriend him. You must become friends with roid heads like him because they are gonna be handling the shit you'll be jacking into your ass with a needle, and you don't want a stranger, or, even worse, an enemy in that position. It's easy to fuck with the contents of steroid bottles, so treat the muscle-heads as you would a bitter server at an Applebee's. BE NICE SO THEY DON'T FUCK WITH YOUR SHIT!

After you have become friends, ask if he can hook you up. He will. He will also charge you roughly 20 - 40 percent commission on your steroid purchase, depending on how stupid you are and how well you befriended him. Get your roids in an awkward exchange one day in the gym parking lot. Go home excited as hell, but nervous that your heart may explode. By the way, you are old enough now to get a physical and talk to your doctor prior to starting a steroid cycle: you are not a 21-year-old Italian guy, so do what's right. Now, being very aware of your cardio-pulmonary status and hoping that your heart won't explode, shoot that first shot into your ass. If you have a wife and kids, you should hide this from them. What the hell kind of role model are you, Johnny mid-life crisis??? OK, no judgment here. Just don't let them know.

Now hit the gym. Rinse with steroids and repeat for six to eight weeks. You will notice your body changing by leaps and bounds. You will also notice your mental outlook becoming bleak. You are 35 and had a life and now you are going through all the same feelings of inadequacy which accompanied puberty. LOSER, LOSER, LOSER (your brain will be yelling this throughout this crisis; ignore it). You will have rage issues. These rage issues will be different from when you were a teenager and only had walls and girlfriends to hit. Now you actually have worthwhile possessions you can damage: a car, kids, a wife you hate . . . DON'T THINK THAT, DO NOT THINK THAT! She loves you and you love her, it's the damn Winstrol/Dianabol combo kicking in. Whenever you feel like raging, get out of the house. Drag your ripped 40-something body into your mid-life-crisis-mobile and drive. Honk your horn a lot as people cut you off, yell at people in SUVs who look like they may be from the West Indies. Curse out pedestrians. Holler things at minivans with families in them like, "I GOT A GOOD MIND TO COME OVER THERE AND RAPE YOU WITH YOUR OWN DAUGHTER'S DICK!" This will let them know that you are lacking logic and are clearly insane. Let the car take your rage. Try to not kill anyone. If you do kill someone you will probably be fine in terms of the law, since you haven't been drinking. If you have been drinking throughout your steroid cycle, you are an imbecile and your liver is worse off than a Russian organ donor with a Stolichnaya intravenous drip.

Now you're back in shape. Every day is a battle for your sanity, but hey—your love handles are gone. You may feel tempted to leave your wife and kids and move in with the hot stripper you've been banging unprotected that you met at the gym. DO NOT DO THIS! The drugs have influenced your ego. Merely know that you are the man again; you could still demand street cred even though you are 10 years from retirement. Wean yourself off the drugs, change your phone number, and switch gyms to lose the stripper and let her go back to fucking her dirty uncle. Take your family on a cruise or vacation to somewhere warm to make it up to them for being such a self-indulgent loser and to show off your abs for the last time in your life. Well done, gentleman: you were selfish yet still caring in the end. Most pro athletes in your position are out raping and making dogs fight for money. You are better than a professional athlete. You got through steroids with no felonies. Mazel tov!

Now get some acne cream on your back.

Proper etiquette for pooping your pants as a grown man (a true tale)

It is not easy to be a gentleman while possessing slovenly swamp ass. But know this, as we grow up we become more infant-like in several ways; most notably, we long to suckle a nice supple breast, and, on occasion, we shit ourselves. Shitting ourselves may happen at all-inclusive resorts where we are smart enough to spend our hard-earned, first-world money in a third-world haven full of child prostitutes who may look close enough to 18 to not trouble us morally. Sometimes, the ice cubes in a drink may send us spiraling in Montezuma's revenge, while other times the undercooked chicken at a beachfront BBQ romp may get our bowels in a gravy-like state. However, my incontinence stems from wanting to stay slender.

I am not anally bulimic; however, I drink less beer, which has given me a fetish for red wine. Just because I am a connoisseur does not mean I can't put the booze away like I did when I was 25. So I may go through 12 - 15 glasses of red wine in a night. Usually I am aware enough to excuse myself from my peers and pound the liters of fermented grapes out of my asshole in a muddy porcelain wrecking mess. However, other times I need to socialize and can't be running off to the loo every eight minutes.

One night, I was working at a very prestigious comedy club in New York City (less prestigious once you hear this story). As comics, we drink for free, but we tip well to compensate. Fourteen glasses of cheap Australian cabernet sauvignon into my night, I figured I could squeeze out a fart. I was mistaken. I squeezed out a half pound of dirty shit into my black Calvin Klein's. I always wear black underwear just in case this happens. (I own one pair of white underwear, but they serve the same purpose as canned food at my house - they are there just in case the apocalypse arrives).

I had baggy jeans on, so nobody noticed at first. Problem being, the only people left in the comedy club were comics and staff. I ran casually to the men's room. Usually, I could grab paper towels and "dry-clean" my shit-stained drawers, but this bathroom had no paper towels - only a powerful hand-dryer. I shit the rest of my innards out while hovering over the toilet seat so as not to catch crabs or get my dirt pussy pregnant. My shit sprayed all over the toilet seat. I went to work with the toilet paper and cleaned the seat the best I could. It was not good enough. There was still fecal matter all over the part where the seat connects to the bowl, and I was not wily or trained enough in the janitorial ways of the Cuban to get this out. I was hammered at this point and was very aware of how long I had been in the bathroom. I needed to hurry or club management would know it was me, or so I thought.

My underpants were beyond repair. Shit. There was no garbage can in this bathroom because there were no paper towels. I threw my sopping wet, diarrhea-soaked Calvin's behind the toilet and bare-balled the rest of the night. I left the club quickly, went to another bar, did a shot and then threw up red wine all over this bar's toilet. I went home in a cab. In retrospect, there was nothing I could have done. Hopefully, when you shit your pants in a work environment, you are high enough on the food chain to fire the witnesses. I was not. I did my best. However, I don't work that comedy club anymore. Not by choice. They know it was me. I will let a few months pass, or hope the booker dies in a head-on car crash.

Then I will go back and restore my gentlemanly name.

Proper etiquette for rebounding after a relationship with a girl you thought you loved (or actually loved)

Once in a while, we meet a woman who sweeps us off our feet. She is equal parts sexy, intelligent (for a woman, which means she may have majored in "poli-sci"), can cook, clean, listen, be minimally intrusive, and converse easily. This may be a trick. Many women fear being alone and growing old, even if they are fat, single, cat-owning lesbians who perform comedy or folk music while sweating profusely. So, on occasion women can fake all of these qualities in order to get and keep a man. We can usually read these fake-out actions, although it may take years to realize that we've been bamboozled. If your woman is checking your things, doesn't trust you, or is getting in the way of your career after she told you she "wanted you to be successful," it's time to let her go.

As men, we are not good at breakups. We have fears that we may not be able to do better, so we waver to and fro on our decision to cohabitate. Eventually, we act like assholes, just enough to push our women away so that they break up with us. It is not a very honorable thing to do, but in the end it is the most gentlemanly thing to do. Women say they like honesty, but that's only until they're about to get booted out onto the cold, hard streets and they have to go stay with their sisters for a while. Let your woman break up with you, always. You will be an asshole to a certain degree, but at least she will have ended it.

Now, for the easy part; run out on the streets and express your exultation. Sing your freedom from the rooftops. Have sex, go for walks, enjoy music again, listen to Simon and Garfunkel . . . oh shit, here comes the sadness. You have now realized that sex, food, booze, drugs, and old 70s tunes do not fill the void of a broken heart. Even though you were sure that your relationship was bad, it now seems like an abusive relationship is better than no relationship. YOU ARE ALONE! How to rebound? Take interest in things outside of yourself. Find new hobbies, begin to create, and start doing something with your meaningless existence. Focus on work and focus on well being. This will start to attract other women to you. They may not all be "A"-type chicks, but take what you can get to help you regain your self esteem.

Do not bang chicks at work. It seems easy, but it will only hinder your progress as a gentleman down the road. You may fuck chicks in your workplace, but make sure that they are imported from other workplaces and are only temporarily in your workplace. Your ex may try to reach out to you. Do not have sex with her. Do not meet with her. YOU ARE TOO BUSY AND TOO SUCCESSFUL FOR THIS BULLSHIT!!! You may talk to her on the telephone to help her get over missing you, but don't go too deep. You may say that you "miss her too," but make sure that you don't mean it. Do not feel that you have to jump back into a relationship with anybody. Try being friends with a woman before you fuck her. She will probably think that you're half a faggot, but fuck it.

Be friends with a bunch of women. Many of them will begin to cluster around you, thinking that you are the perfect man, and it's probably because, right now, you are. This equation of uncertain circumstances has led you to this place. Soon you will forget all about your ex, and then you will see her out with another man. Hopefully, he will not be a professional black athlete. Regardless of who he is, your first thought will be "they can't be having sex, they are probably just friends." THIS THOUGHT IS DEAD WRONG; SHE HAS MOVED ON! She is getting plowed nine ways to

Wednesday because even though you may have banged before your breakup, it was passionless sex and was usually either missionary or doggie. It was not good. This guy is doing shit to your ex that is illegal in most of Dubai (that could actually just be kissing without a burqa - HE IS PROBABLY DOING ASS-PLAY WITH HER).

Be as polite as you can. Give her a hug, shake this loser's hand, and go about your day, by which I mean call up a girl who was just your friend until now. Don't tell her that you saw your ex, but go out for drinks with her. Get hammered. Live in her labia for a week or so. By now, you will have forgotten about your slimy ex who had moved on before you even knew she had ended it with you. In the end, you come out looking like a champ to your ex. Once she breaks up with this tool, she may call you again to ask where you left the Preparation H so she can fix the ramifications from her pro-athlete ass-play. Be polite and go back to your stable of "new car-scented" vaginas. Rinse and repeat. Do this until you fall in love again and have to do it all over.

Remember, gentleman, life is a cycle.

Proper etiquette for dating a feminist

Feminists are not as rare of a breed as you may think. They still exist and in growing numbers. Although we think that the world as a playing field may have already been leveled, many women still compare their relative places in society to that of presidents and other great war-mongers. They want to hold positions at the top of the food chain, and many women do so within the masculine confines of show business, fundraising, and rape culture. These women may be intimidating at first glance. They will be well put together, will appear stronger than most women, and will have an air of arrogance about them. Do not be scared off by these women. You are at an age where you have already completed the dumb, hot, blonde "trifecta." You need a strong woman. Don't be afraid of these women, for if you are, it signifies that you are afraid of the deepest feminine parts of yourself. Yes, we all have a little bit of feminine inside of us.

First of all, you must find a feminist. You can do this at a pro-choice rally, any kind of hippie event, or a Sarah McLachlan concert. DO NOT CONFUSE YOUR FEMINIST WITH A LESBIAN! Many feminists have dabbled in lesbianism and many lesbians are feminists, but you want a feminist who has already ridden out her lesbian phase. A common misconception about feminists is that they want to be the man in all of their relationships; they don't. A feminist will not pick you up for dates, open your car door, or pay for dinner. She wants all of the perks that go with being a damsel in distress with the added bonus of being mentally in charge. So you will still have to foot the bill for this relationship.

Wine and cheese and a talk is a good first date. Play coy sexually with your femi-Nazi. Pretend that sex with her is the last thing on your mind. Even when she invites you into her home for sex, turn her down. This will make her question her world view. You have gone from being this virile, rape-loving male to a soft-sweet man that she must care for. You have made her question all of Erica Jong's works.

When you do get to sex, pretend that you want her to be in charge. This will unleash her inner beast. She will be a freak in bed. She may have hairy armpits and a hairy bush because she is holding onto all of the emotional baggage she had from her Indigo Girl lesbian days. She probably uses some kind of granola for deodorant. This will change the longer your relationship lasts. You will discover that underneath this hard shell of a woman is a timid little girl who wants to be loved.

Now you must make her pay for meals and make her feel as if she is the sexual aggressor. Soon, she will want you to meet her family, and she will want to get into a serious relationship with you. Gone will be the days of her being independent and not giving a shit about how you spend your time. She will now want to know where you are all the time. She may even start to check your phone and your emails, and she may quit her spoken word/improvisational troupe.

Merely by dating a feminist, you have turned her into a "masculinist." If every gentleman did this with about five feminists, soon there will be no feminists left in the world. Next step: a puppet woman president. You have done your part to remedy sexism.

Well done, gentleman.

Proper etiquette for banging a much older lady

The elderly have earned a position in society as meek, tender, and approachable. Oftentimes, they seem confused, and we tend to think of them as washed up, crushed vessels for failed dreams and the tangled proteins of Alzheimer's disease. But older women have attained a certain renaissance nowadays. Due to the influx of yoga, Pilates, and healthier eating, women are staying "fuckable" even into their late 60s. As modern-day degenerate gentlemen, it behooves us to bang a couple of these older women before they find their final resting places six feet under and become worm food as their children and grandchildren cry over their caskets.

Women 20 or 30 years older than you may seem like they are fragile pieces of tail, but in reality these women know more about what they like than any 20-year-old you will enter. There will be major differences in the vaginal regions. For example, if you are bedding a 20-something who has not yet had her slut phase or hasn't been with a black man, you will notice that more times than not the post-teen still has her vagina inside of her. You will have to do some digging around to find what you are looking for; the clit may seem to be hidden under some labia-like drapes. In contrast, an older woman, who has probably had dozens of lovers, fucked a good rock band, and popped out a few mistakes (children) pre-divorce, will have a vagina which is far easier to navigate, as it will be hanging halfway down her hamstrings.

On paper, the "outie" vagina is not as attractive, but it gets the job done. Another positive to women in their 60s is that most of them are sterile. This may be by choice (i.e., getting tubes tied after their three children went on to do nothing but eat up finances from a divorce settlement), or because of some kind of fallopian tube/uterus disease, or due to severe vaginal scraping as a result of multiple abortions. Either way, this makes birth control a non-issue. We all know as degenerate gentlemen that nothing beats coming inside of a warm, wet hole. This is much less problematic with an elder stateswoman than it is with a woman in her 20s looking to trap you with an unwanted pregnancy.

If you accidentally pop one off inside of a hipster pussy, you will run around frantically looking for pennies to feed the woman or Coca-Cola to flush her yam out, and you may even go as far as having to shell out 40 bucks for a morning-after pill. With an older woman, just bust your loads and let her drip out squatting by the bedside. Older women are usually much more financially secure than their younger predecessors, so put your credit card away - dinner is on your Phyllis Diller look-alike.

Maybe you don't think that older women are hot. Well, you've been looking at the wrong ones. Jack off to a Katey Sagal rape scene on Sons of Anarchy, and your cock will get right back in the game. Older women also love the taste of cum, as it reminds them of the days when they were moving up the career ladder at a rapid rate until they hit that sociological glass ceiling. So get ready for a lot of swallowing, which will help keep your laundry costs down. More cum in a woman's throat equals less cum on your sheets - hence, less time at the laundromat: simple arithmetic. Once you cross the bridge into retired pussy, you can always come back to level playing-field pussy, but the journey is worth it.

Here's how to hook up with an older woman. You will need to position yourself in a geographic location where older women are found. South Florida is a good bet for this. Get on a golf course or a tennis court. These women will still be fit and fuckable.

Even though they may possess liver spots, they still have the common sense to take care of their bodies. These women also still have friends, as they are out in public and not merely decaying in some assisted-living program. These women also have disposable income, as they are out playing one of two sports which are still associated with the middle and upper classes of America. The fact that they have friends means that they want to be better than their friends, and that's where having the badge of honor which is fucking a man 20 - 25 years their junior comes into play. This means that your game does not have to be as strong as it is with a younger woman, because Gladys has something to prove to her friends.

Approach her in public, when she is with her friends. Be overtly sexual but do not mention sex; rely strongly on innuendo. At no point should you mention the difference in age. Flatter her and all of her friends, and then ask for her number once you have separated her from the herd. She will give it to you. You can probably call her that night. Even if she did have plans for the evening, it would be eating an early-bird dinner at 4:30 pm, watching something on CBS, and falling asleep with a lemon zinger tea, some lubricant, and a 12-year-old vibrator. No longer will she need that tool, as she will have yours.

Go over to her place. Take a bottle of wine. Old women like white wine. You will feel gay as shit drinking white wine, but you will feel less gay in half an hour when you are balls deep in a woman that went to high school with Moses. Drink the wine and chat about intellectual things. Do not bring up her past divorces, emotional hardships, or what it was like to walk 12 miles each way to school in a time before the wheel was invented. Take her into the bedroom once the time is right. Kiss her passionately. DO NOT TREAT HER ANY DIFFERENTLY AS A LOVER! GO AT HER FULL TILT BOOGIE! Think of the relaxation she is feeling every time your dick enters her. YOU ARE A HERO! You are doing the Lord's work. People should wear poppies in November for what you have done.

She will have a great time. She should orgasm. When she does, she will squirt, tremble, shiver, and cry all at the same time. This means she is free once again. You can bang her again and again. Remember, you are a beast in the bed when it comes to women who haven't fucked since Kurt Cobain sucked on a shotgun. Give her a pillow to drip out on. One word of caution: if this woman is promiscuous, she probably has chlamydia, which is rampant among elderly women. This will be something you can hold over her head for financial gain later in the relationship if she is still alive in 10 days (which is usually how long it takes for chlamydia to kick in full force). You can sleep over and have her blow you in the morning. It is not inappropriate for you to ask for 300 dollars for cab fare. She will think that 300 dollars is a lot for a cab, but what does she know? SHE USED TO PAY A NICKEL FOR A CANDY BAR! Explain the notion of inflation in a fledgling economy to her.

You now have a regular booty call that you can put on your phone. If you forget her name, just put her under "well marinated," because her pussy definitely is marinated. Try to avoid being seen with "well marinated" in public unless you want to use her as bait to get back into dating girls your own age; whenever they see you with an older woman, they will naturally think that you just have a very close relationship with your grandmother.

Well done, gentleman: you have won on all counts.

Proper etiquette for cheating on your wife/girlfriend

First off, I in no way advocate cheating or "philandering," as a more educated man (who never gets any pussy) would call it. I HAVE NEVER CHEATED ON ANY OF MY GIRLFRIENDS! And that is exactly the attitude that you have to keep going into a cheat. This is all a fantasy world; there is no truth here. Cheating is the exact opposite of the way a gentleman should live his life. Life is truth. Cheating is the blurred lines outside of truth. The only instance in which cheating is altruistic is when your female has behaved in such a way that she deserves to be hit. Now as we all know, women cannot be hit by men. This is not a gentlemanly pursuit, smacking women around. We leave that for hillbillies, uneducated Neanderthals, and financially flush, eleventh-grade dropouts who work the oil rigs in Fort McMurray. Rather than turning on our females physically, we turn on them in "another physical manner" that is both consensual and coital.

First, you must have a horrific argument with your life partner. She may say things like, "Does that make you want to hit me, huh asshole?" No matter what, keep your cool. Like Denzel said, "You wanna go home or you wanna go to jail?" You wanna go home when this is over. NOW LEAVE THE HOUSE ASAP! Your chick will start calling your phone immediately, yelling and leaving messages about how big of an asshole you are. Just walk or drive away and cool off. You being away from her and being so calm is upsetting her more and more. That is what you want. You want her to get so hurtful and angry that she drives you to the brink of questioning the relationship. There is no faking this. She must hurt you in order to earn the cheat. A cheat is a betrayal. But if the betrayal is warranted, a cheat is nothing more than reparations. That's what you're aiming for in this initial fallout, the right to earn payback. And your payback is going to be some fresh pussy.

After a few hours or a day or a week, you may go home. Your female partner will be nothing if not apologetic. Take her apology, accept it, but not deep in your heart. Go about your life for a while. It may take weeks, months, or even years; but soon you will have a business trip. Go on this trip. Now the fences have been mended between you and your partner, so you don't have to worry about her cheating on you while you're away. Fly first class. You deserve it. If she asks why you spent so much . . . WHY THE FUCK ARE YOU LETTING HER LOOK AT YOUR CREDIT CARD CHARGES??? YOU PAY THE BILLS!!! MAN UP!!!

Go to the airport lounge first and have a few high-end drinks. Get on your flight and watch the poor plebes who don't know how to cheat walk to the back of the plane like the losers they are. Have some champagne. Talk to and meet business contacts and women executives that one day you may go out with. Do not call your wife/girlfriend; THIS IS MAN TIME! Take a limo to the hotel when you land. Meet women, have drinks, do whatever business shit you came here to do. Make sure that you have a nice suite. Call and check in with your wife/ girlfriend and tell her you are having fun and blah blah blah . . . MAKE UP WHATEVER SHIT THE PSYCHO WANTS TO HEAR! Then go fuck the fucking hell out of some slut. Tell her lies about where you're from, your name, your age, everything. Wear a condom and come on the drapes. Enjoy it.

When you are done, shower off and fight the urge to call your wife/girlfriend. You will wake up the next morning and pretend nothing happened. GOOD, BECAUSE NOTHING DID HAPPEN! Hopefully, you were smart and banged a total classless whore or somebody else in a relationship. Lie to yourself about this cheat. That's why most good cheats are never found out, because gentlemen can lie to themselves. Don't even bother calling your wife/girlfriend yet. She doesn't deserve it. She may come pick you up at the airport if she wants to. See, now wasn't that better than hitting her in a fit of rage? Relationship saved! You can do this anytime your wife/girlfriend gets out of line emotionally. Also, make sure you don't bring her back a souvenir from the business trip; this will only make her suspicious.

Proper etiquette for dealing with a clingy girl that you had a threesome with

We all love looking back fondly on our threesome experiences. We have become good friends with the guy that we shared that girl with. Usually we want our threesomes to be "never-again" circumstances, mainly because once we have shared bodily fluids and pumped many loads down a woman's throat, we do not want to see that woman again in any kind of social context. You may have great memories of such a woman naked, her feet caressing your balls (if that's your thing), her singing, telling you about her poetry and her multimedia commissioned art pieces, but then there may come a day when you have to see this woman without two penises inside of her. You will barely recognize her at first.

Usually this post-three-way whore sighting can be avoided by only having three-ways with tourists or girls who are leaving the city in which you fornicated with them. Sometimes this cannot be controlled. You may find out that the woman you used as a conduit for friendship via a rotisserie-style maneuver works close to the place you work. Now all bets are off. You will be out one night and see her on the street. You will be without your buddy with whom you banged her a week ago. You will have to make small talk and be polite, because even though the sex was consensual, you don't know how crazy this woman actually is.

She may go cry rape to the authorities if she doesn't feel like a woman after that night of debauchery that you shared. So make small talk with her. Try to learn her name at some point. Tell her that you are interested in the things that she is talking about. Promise that you will text her. She will ask what you're doing now. This means that she wants to go back to your place and have sex. Don't fall for this trap! THIS BITCH IS CLINGY AS FUCK! YOU NEED TO GET OUT OF THERE! Hopefully, you are sober. If not, you may be horny and picturing her swallowing your goop. GET OUT OF THERE! Remember, this girl banged your filthy friend and you at the same time. Not only is she not girlfriend material, she is not solo fucking material. Tell her again that you will text her. DO NOT TEXT HER! Put her on your contact list as "three-way girl." At some point you must learn her name in case this happens again. Hug her and get the fuck out of Dodge. That was easy enough, right? WRONG!

A day or two will pass and then you will get a text from a gay friend who is working in Greenwich Village. His text will say, "The girl you had a threesome with is looking for you." Many thoughts will enter your mind. At first you will wonder, "Is this bitch pregnant?" Then you will realize that you smartly wore condoms (against your better judgment) on that fateful night. You will also remember that all of your ejaculate landed in her mouth. So you're good on that count. Mouth babies are not a real thing. Text your gay friend back and say, "Tell her I'll call her tomorrow." You will not call her the next day, but you have to at least text her. Text some small talk. Expect a "winky" face or a happy face in return from her. Let her have this moment.

There, now that should be done, right? Nope! You'll go out to another bar and hear that she was there looking for you. Apparently, this girl is checking out all the places that you frequent. You're fucked now. This is some straight-up Fatal Attraction bullshit. Why couldn't she be attracted to the other guy from the threesome? I'll tell you why, because he is ugly as fuck and looks like Matisyahu with Down syndrome. You were the hot guy in the three-way, and you have way more going for you career-wise. Also, you have seen the inside of a gym, and the other guy needs more dental work than most Holocaust survivors. AVOID THIS WOMAN!

Over, right? Wrong, you will see her on the street again. She'll tell you that she wants to hang out with you again. She will also mention that she isn't the clingy type. This is a flat-out lie. SHE IS THE CLINGY TYPE! Who says that?? "I'm not the clingy type." Mention that you heard that she was out looking for you. This should turn her off, right? Wrong! SHE IS A CLINGY PSYCHO! GET OUT OF THERE!

Now, it's done. Unfortunately, part of being a gentleman by its very definition is that you are a man. A day will pass, and then you will get horny. You will call her and fuck her. You have let yourself and the rest of the world down. The very best that you can hope for now is that you fuck her poorly so that she never wants to see you again. This may work. Make sure that you are impotent for most of the sex. Good luck being a man and evading clingy bitches.

It's tough, because gentlemen love attention.

Proper etiquette for having a friend bang an older woman to get you a six-figure contract

Those of us who consider ourselves creative will often face financial difficulties. Until we have that moment where we break out as international celebrities, we will constantly have to deal with the fact that we don't know where that next chunk of change is coming from. Luckily, we find ways to get by; residuals, sound exchange royalties, and public appearances can round out the schedule of a modern-day degenerate man. If you are not a creative degenerate, you probably have a job that has crushed most of your dreams and desire, but there is still hope. There are several older women who are incredibly disgusting both on a physical and spiritual level. Many of these older women attempt to relive the failures of their past by associating with promising younger talents.

These ladies try to buy their way into show business by hanging with C-level talents who appear to be desperate. Now you may not consider yourself C-level talent, but if you aren't wealthy and are in need of getting a six-figure deal from a disgusting older woman, you are C-level talent at best. A good place to find these "hungry for fame" older women is wherever talent gathers. She could be on the lookout for singers, actors, or comedians.

Put yourself into one of these types of venues. You will meet her. She will look like a hobbit or a troll or some kind of Star Wars character. She will be smelly, and you will want to throw up a soup-like substance any time you get within a 12-foot radius of this woman. But keep the end goal in mind. You want a six-figure deal so that you can go to New York, do your one-man show, and explode to the next level (or something that six figures can buy). Other less-talented people will already be clamoring for attention from this "Elder Philanthropist of Finance," but remember that you are the best of the worst and you deserve it the most.

Find out her back story. She probably was an only child and, as a result of her horrific ugliness, her parents spoiled her and gave her everything that she could ever want except for real happiness. She now owns several properties in a major metropolitan center, and she has many young lovers who don't know any better. She probably gives them a warm bed to sleep in and the opportunity to fuck her "mangled urine dumpster" and think that they are players. You will not be entering this old excuse for a piss hole, as you are a gentleman. One day you will have a chat with this grizzled, rich pussy owner and she will mention that she wants to help fund your dream. In this regard, she is somewhat of an angel. Now look at her face . . . less of an angel.

She will make arrangements for you to fly to NYC to look at theatres and have meetings with publicists; if that goes well, she may sign a deal with you. THIS IS A BIG DEAL! A year ago you were waiting tables at Planet Hollywood or some other corporate restaurant, and all you ever wanted was to get out of the waiter game and prove that you could hang with the big boys. This deal can get you there. Fly to New York with her and be on your best behavior. You are staying in different hotels and you are happy about that because you don't even want French tourists to think that you're banging somebody's autistic grandmother. Some people may think that you kidnapped this woman from an assisted-living facility and you are spending the rest of her fortune before she dies in a cold, loveless bed. Try to avoid people thinking that.

During your days in NYC, you will have to meet up with this woman and go look at theatres. She will buy you dinner and drinks. Day three, you will finally decide on a theatre. It will be midtown and mere moments from Times Square, the center of the universe. You begin to get excited. Your dreams are coming true. Within a few days, you will be out of the waiter game and will be developing a solo show that is Broadway-bound. You are exhausted from walking all day. You stop in at your hotel, and this unsweetened sugar mama says that she needs to use your bathroom. You may let her use your bathroom; after all, she is paying for all of this shit.

While the sound and stench of her steamy piss (which probably smells like asparagus and geriatric meds) fills your ears and nose, she yells out, "So what do you think? You ready to see my old twat?" You yell back, "I'll be in the lobby." You got out of this, or so you think. After she wipes her disgusting, rash-filled undercarriage, she comes down to the lobby and tells you that she very much believes in you and wants to support your endeavor financially. However, she says, "I came to New York to get laid, and I don't care if it's you or somebody else, but I may not be able to sign a contract if I don't get laid . . . just saying." Tell her that you will meet her for a celebratory dinner at Smith and Wollensky Steakhouse. Make some calls.

Find your old friend who is a comic that lives in NYC. Tell him about your dilemma. He is probably single since he is a raging alcoholic and a comedian. Tell him that you're going to get him laid and get him a free dinner accompanied by high-end wine. Do not tell him how disgusting the woman is. That's what the wine is for; if he drinks enough wine he may be able to find some beauty in this woman's soulless carcass. Meet your friend at the restaurant an hour before the urine-scented Yankee candle that is the sugar mama shows up. Get booze into him quickly.

The woman will show up, and she will look less bad than she did before you both started drinking. Some of her inner ugliness has become kindness because of the financial potential she represents to you. Have steak, have laughs, and get hammered. The bill will arrive, and it will be in the ballpark of 1,400 dollars. At some point, the older woman will get up to use the facilities or to empty her colostomy bag. She may think that you will pick up the bill when she is in the ladies room rubbing Gold Bond or some kind of anti-inflammatory ointment onto her crotch. SHE IS WRONG! Use this time to make sure that your friend is fully onboard to fuck this ancient hog. Tell him that you'll owe him one.

When the senile wench returns, excuse yourself and let these kids have their fun. Give her a peck on the cheek and tell her that you'll meet at noon tomorrow for your flight home. Your friend will follow through on banging "Nana," not because he wants to help you so much, but because he is a degenerate and thinks that there might be some kind of story in this that he can eventually use for his comedy. HE IS WRONG! He will regret this day. In fact, after banging her, he will re-examine his life, realize that he is an alcoholic, and will go into recovery and get sober.

The next day you will see your dementia-riddled dream sponsor and she will tell you that she had a great time and is ready to go home and sign the deal. You did it; you're going to NYC with a one-man show.

Call your friend to thank him. He won't answer. He is going through a severe breakdown followed by depression and several relapses. He will call you in a month. Nice, dude. Repay him one day with a shitty road gig. This woman will sign the contract and then show her anti-Semitic side and try to back out because she doesn't like dealing with Jewish managers. She will never make it in show business. All the good managers are Jewish. You will sue her and get 15 grand. Looks like you'll have to make it to NYC on your own, but hey - you got a great story, 15 grand, and you never had to fuck that walking catheter. Also, in the long run you helped turn your friend's life around.

Well done, gentleman!

Proper etiquette for changing your look for a gay-friendly world

As we age, we have to face certain degenerate truths. We are not where we wanted to be career-wise, we have not found the love of our life yet, we are not as rich or famous as we thought that we would be, we are flawed in ways that only 12-step programs can ameliorate, and finally, the best of our days are clearly behind us. So what can we do to change the inevitable truth that we are becoming elders in a society with no morality and far too much globalization? We can start to change some of our habits. This is easier said than done. We are creatures of repetition. What worked in our 20s won't work now, but we are too dumb to change. So let's start easily.

We love our old ripped jeans and our t-shirts and our black underwear because they don't show the skids that collect due to our beer shits and horrible diet. But we need to evolve. A new look will change your life. At first people will make fun of not seeing you in a scrubby Bon Jovi concert t-shirt, but soon you will see that you are now dating outside of your previous pussy league. An image change will not only get you more and better pussy, but it will open up new opportunities for financial gain and broaden your career trajectory. Now, unless God made you wrong in the eyes of the political right and you're gay, you probably have no idea what fashion is. Most straight men think that fashion is a week that happens every year in most major cities, with a bunch of skinny models who live on a diet of nicotine and wet Kleenex. We think that fashion is something that only weird Euro-trash half-fags can pull off. We walk by store windows and see well-put-together outfits and think, "What kind of glory-hole party could I wear that to?"

Well, in case you haven't gotten the memo or turned on a television in the past 15 years, GAY IS EVERYWHERE! It's not only okay to dress like a "gay-lord," it is in fact applauded in most first and second-world countries. So let your preconceptions go and let's faggot up our wardrobe. We have no idea where to start, but luckily most men's stores are staffed by gay men. Gay men love to work retail because it allows them the flexible hours to pursue their dreams of being singers/dancers. In addition, they get great discounts and can accordingly wardrobe themselves for their auditions and gay encounters at night in public parks and rest stops.

So go into a store. Not a Gap, please. Leave that for struggling Asian students who are trying to look Americanized. Find a Banana Republic or a J Crew, or, if you lack the musculature to look like a real man and instead resemble Tilda Swinton, you can go into a Zara. Avoid Armani Exchange, as most of their stuff has logos and their look is more Guido than fag. Now, theoretically "Guidos" can be fags, although they are usually closeted. However, you are attempting to look gay, not closeted gay. The closet gay look will get you compliments from closeted gay "Guidos," and you want to avoid any kind of conversation with these greasy "wanna-be" queers.

Walk into the store and leave your ego at the door. Walk up to a minority gay man. Black or Spanish will work best in this case. The fact that you chose a double minority gay man over a white gay man speaks volumes about your liberalism and will work in your favor, because double minorities have to work harder to prove themselves in the workplace. Go up to the double minority gay man. Do not call him a double minority gay man, or even a gay man for that matter. Just be jovial and say, "Hi." He will ask if he can help you. He can.

Say this: "I want to change my look and I have no idea where to start. I want to go something like an upscale casual and really want to work outside of my comfort zone."

He will be excited to help your untailored white ass. He will feel like he is doing a cameo role on an old episode of Queer Eye for the Straight Guy. He will show you a combination of vests, jackets, ties, purple shirts, blue shirts, button-downs, sweater vests, dark jeans, leather shoes, and pants that you think are way too tight. You will fit snugly into some of these clothes and will look disturbingly at your gut and your love handles while in the fitting room. You can deal with your male anorexia later. For right now, try on all the clothes.

The gay man will look at you with hope every time you step of the fitting room and into your new and improved, upscale life. Buy at least three different outfits. You will be tired now. You should have spent at least 400 or 500 bucks, but it isn't the financial strain that has exhausted you, it's the fact that straight men are not built for shopping. Thank Lester, or Juan, or Leroy, or whoever the double minority gay man was. Wish him the best on his upcoming audition for Rent, In the Heights, or Kinky Boots. Take your purchases, go home, jack off, and nap. DO NOT THINK ABOUT THE DOUBLE MINORITY GAY SALESMAN WHILE YOU JACK OFF! Also do not think of your bloated midriff that you had to see all afternoon in the fitting room mirror.

After a nap, dress up in your new gear and go out. Go to a bar or some place with cigars and wine. People will be looking at you - gay men, women, old people, black women. It is not because they think you are gay. It is because you look good. Watch what happens with your life now. Things will come to you easier. You will feel better about yourself. You will start dating women who don't need to be hidden from the world. Your dreams will start to come true, one day at a time. You may become addicted to fashion because you realize that when you look good, you feel good. You will get a little giddy-up in your step every time you walk. You may find yourself sober more often than not. You may find yourself getting in better shape than you've ever been. You have gracefully gone from artsy bum to aspiring man on the rise.

Now that you look better, you can also increase your degenerate habits because people will be less inclined to judge you. At first you thought dressing up was gay, but now you see that "gay" is just a word for a better life.

Well done, straight gentleman who is gay-friendly.

Proper etiquette for maintaining a monogamous relationship

For years, we raised the battle cry: "We are men, hear us roar for our freedom." We are not a species that wants to be tied down. We live by the sword and die by the sword. We fought off the weeping women who longed to lock us down. We distracted them from the typical questions: "So are we dating?" "Are we girlfriend/boyfriend?" "Are we just friends?" "I can deal with that! Just please tell me?" THEY CANNOT

DEAL WITH THAT! They want to know that you are exclusive and they do not give a shit that you may have just gotten out of a relationship and that you may have been cheated on by a whore from Prince Edward Island. They do not give a shit about your baggage. They just need somebody who can accept and deal with the bipolar behavioral aspects of their baggage. So we choose to be single.

Occasionally, we shack up with a lady because the sex is good or she has provided us with a comfortable enough lifestyle that we don't need to stray. But soon, we tire of being kept and we run like Bruce Springsteen lyrics toward Single-Ville, USA. However, once in a while we get a scare. We have a glimpse of death and think, "Man, I don't want to die alone. Who will call the ambulance when I collapse in the solarium in South Florida?" Or we have a near-STD/pregnancy experience with some random trollop and we think, "That's it, I'm outta the game. I'm cashing in my chips while I'm still alive." We find nice girls and settle down and give them our bodies, our minds, and our souls. We turn everything over to them and promise MONOGAMY.

At first this will be a magical feeling. We will convince ourselves that we have given up our old ways and that we have found love. We have uncovered this feeling that so many poets and singers and artists have used as a muse throughout history. We are MEN in a different way than we ever thought possible. We are abiding by the laws of traditional society. We are off the market. We have one thing in our lives that is now a constant. Monogamy makes rejection, failure, and aspiration all take a back seat to the constant thing in our lives: one woman. We can now have unprotected sex and not just because we're drunk. We will lie in bed after sex and not think, "How do I get this woman out of here?"

We will actually enjoy being with our women. We will go out in public, and other women will pick up on the fact that we are faithful. This will attract other women to us, but we will have no need for these other women because we are monogamists. We will learn to accept the flaws in our partners as they accept the flaws in us. We will notice how minimal our own flaws are, in comparison to our partners' flaws. We will think "Holy shit, this person is flawed." But then we will commend ourselves and hold ourselves up as martyrs for being so willing to deal with the flaws of our partners.

We are great people to be able to pull off monogamy. Why did we rail so long against love when it is such a self-fulfilling pursuit? Even though we have love for another person, we are making ourselves feel better by giving this love. Then temptation will rear its ugly head. We will then begin to resent our partners for holding us back. We remember the days when we were carefree and would be with up to four partners at once. We remember how our creativity thrived in our Jim Morrison-like days. This will all happen within the first month. In order to stay monogamous, there are rules.

Women are not okay simply with the fact that you don't have sexual contact with other women. They want more than simple, sexual dedication. You will have to let all of your women friends fall by the wayside; because all of these women who were just friends clearly want to sleep with you (according to your woman). She has these thoughts because she knows that all of her "man friends" want to fuck her, and these "man friends" view you as an impediment to them fucking her. This causes further resentment between both of you. But soon, you will be tricked and agree that you and your partner are "best friends and lovers." So why do you need other friends? This is her argument, and you fall victim to it in the name of being a bigger person and respecting the prison that is monogamy.

Soon, you will have cost yourself career options by cutting several woman friends out of your life. Now, you are alone with this devil woman who cares nothing for your hopes or your dreams but claims that she only wants the best for you. The sex, which was initially great because it was unprotected, will now occur less and less. Foreplay will have left the playing field altogether, and you will both only fuck when you truly feel that it is necessary. Both of you will feel like you're doing each other a favor. STAY STRONG! While you fuck, you will both be thinking of other partners, usually people that you work with. Do not let her onto this ruse. KEEP YOUR EYES CLOSED AS YOU CLIMAX TO WHATEVER BULKY WAITRESS YOU ARE FANTASIZING ABOUT! Your partner will do the same as she thinks about a blacker guy or a younger guy and occasionally a hot woman.

The sex will become intolerable to the point that you will begin to look forward to your time alone so that you can masturbate. You will go online and find women who look like the women you wish you could be banging instead of the woman you have signed your life away to. You are now in monogamy purgatory. Beat your dick often. This will help extend the length of your monogamous relationship. The length of your relationship will be important for when you rebound out of this. New women will respect the fact that you stayed with the previous woman for at least four months. Soon, you and your partner will be done. You did it. You had a monogamous relationship. Now you know why tribes which thrived in the past fought and died for polygamy. Polygamy is sanity.

Once you have broken off with your monogamous partner, you will both go your own way and have fuck festivals. You will wonder who she is fucking. He will probably be better looking and much more successful than you, because monogamy has siphoned all of your energy. You will rebound with a fat waitress whose vagina smells like spoiled milk and Czechoslovakian armpits. Regardless, you are back in the game. Now get your shit together and start dating "six and a halves" again. Do not fall into the monogamy trap until you have another STD scare. This is how life will go for a while. Soon you will be 45 and have to decide whether it may be worth it to turn gay.

Consult me again at that point.

Proper etiquette for attending a big girl party

The rise of the healthy female in liberal society has been astounding. LuLu Lemon has given a whole sense of fashion to the modern woman. No longer merely concerned with being skinny and looking like meth-riddled models, women want to be healthy and let their looks follow. Pilates, bikram yoga, and spinning are all on the agendas of big-city girls who want to feel as good as they look. These women have embraced the gluten-free, wheatgrass way of meditative life. They watch their diets and they frequent laser hair removal studios to keep their bodies as polished as their souls. These are the women with which we may want to settle down for a bit. They are attractive, balanced, and high-maintenance. They are marriage material for men with good jobs, strong incomes, and high self-esteem. They are the great unknown frontier for most of us.

To keep a woman of this ilk, we need to have ourselves in top running order, and that's not always easy to do. The demands of being a degenerate male dictate that we take the road less traveled. This means not settling for "good" when "odd" is an option. Thankfully, God made many types of women, and we can choose between skanks, sluts, whores, tubby waitresses, insane hippies, or big girls. Big girls are not marriage material. They are not even dating material, but every once in a while they make a great night out. These well-nourished, herded cattle all gather together one night a month in major, cosmopolitan areas to dance and celebrate their laziness and lack of discipline. They don't acknowledge their failures in empirical beauty; rather they inundate themselves with liquor and claim to be proud of their thyroid problems. This night is called a big girl party.

Now you may be able to find out about these parties online, but the best way to get into one of them is to have a large black friend who is probably a bouncer. He will know almost everybody at the soiree; hence, you can get in for free. You don't want to spend good money at the door; you need to hold onto your cash in case you need to take one of these "heifers" out to a pancake house after an evening of dancing.

First, meet your black bouncer friend at his place of employment. Next, invite a white friend so that you will not be the only white person at this party. It is a very well-known fact that black men love big women. The party will be rife with gangster-type brothers. You want a white guy there just to make it seem like you aren't the only white creep in the world. Take somebody who is the opposite of you. If you are short and muscular, take a tall, fat friend. This will help you stand out if you want to bed one of the "wild buffalos" that you run into later. Meet with your awkward white friend and your black bouncer friend. Have a few drinks to loosen up.

Drive over to the party. You will need to have a car in case these women get hungry later and try to chase you as a food source. A car will ensure your escape to safety. Take small white towels with you. You will need these towels when you enter the club and find out that there is no air conditioning and there are sweaty bovines everywhere. You too, will sweat as there is limited oxygen inside the club, due to these whales selfishly inhaling air. Dab yourself with a white towel. Walk into the club and notice how many looks you get from these slobs. You are nothing but a piece of meat to them. LUCKILY, CANNIBALISM IS ILLEGAL IN MOST STATES!

Go get a Heineken, if there are any left. Remember, this party is frequented by black men. Most of the Heineken, Alize, and Hennessy are probably already eighty-sixed. A Corona may be a better option for you and your white friend. Look around and try to focus on the girls, not the fact that there are more black men in here than the ad-seg yard at Riker's. These black people are all good people, so allow your preconceived notions to fall away. Most of the racial thoughts in your head are media-affected stereotypes and are usually only half truths. That being said, do not start any shit. THESE PEOPLE WILL KILL YOU! YOU WILL DIE!

Go and find a fatty who hasn't been claimed by a brother. Start dancing near her. If she likes you (even though you are white and you can't dance), she will waddle up next to you. She may be attracted to you because you are different than everybody else in the bar. Not only are you white, but you don't smell like a combination of armpit sweat and cocoa butter. Get behind her and grind as the SOCA music blares. You may know some of the words. Feel free to sing. However if the word "nigga" or "nigger" pops up in any of the hip hop tunes, do not sing along at that point. People may be watching your lips move. Grind away. You will feel moistness and smell something that resembles rotten tomato sauce. That is the perspiration from the woman with whom you are dancing. It is gross. Now, you may think of bedding this woman. Then you will think, "Would my bed even hold this woman?" The answer is NO! You will have thoughts pass through your head as your jeans get wet from her "sopping choda" perspiring through her Spanx. You will think, "Can I bang her? Would I be able to stay hard? How would I hide her from the public?" These are all reasonable questions and all reasons that you cannot bang a manatee like this. This lion of the sea with two legs is a walking red flag to your groin. Finish dancing. Look around and find your white goofy friend, who is probably making out with an extra from the movie Soul Plane. Grab him and let him know that you are going to leave. You cannot abandon him here as the only white man. Tell your black bouncer friend that you are out. Get on the subway and go home and shower. It may take a day or two to cleanse your body and a week or two to cleanse your mind. You have experienced the other side without making a huge life mistake. Now log onto YouPorn and beat off to some fatties.

Well done, gentleman!

Proper etiquette for pleasuring yourself in front of two men for money

We all go through phases when we believe ourselves to be martyrs and above all laws of logic. Maybe you're going through a time where you are especially muscular and you just moved out of your parents' house into a cockroach-infested apartment that you got from a friend of yours named Sergio, a male dancer at the strip club where you work. Maybe the year is 1994 and you feel like you need some extra money to help pay your 800-dollar rent. Maybe you're unsure about your sexuality because you are constantly in a workplace surrounded by naked men, and although you are having sex with a ton of women, you feel like you may be overcompensating for your hetero side. You see your other co-workers. Among them are two large black men named Ebony and Hot Chocolate. Ebony is a true entertainer and the essence of a blue-collar male stripper. He often dances to Montell Jordan's 'This is How We Do It.' Hot Chocolate, on the other hand, is a steroid-riddled freak show with a serious ganja habit and a 14-inch penis.

Other strippers that are influencing your current moral compass are Wolf, a homophobic Russian ex-military guy who only strips to supplement his income from renting out pinball machines (yes, pinball machines in 1994); Silver Falcon, a champion bodybuilder who pays for his steroid habit by letting men suck him off for cash; Tommy Zeus, a ripped ex-pimp/crack hustler who lets men suck him off for pleasure, but he justifies it by getting paid; and French Kiss, a hell of a nice guy that you have three-ways and four-ways with but the two of you never discuss sex unless there are women around, yet on occasion when you stay at his place he mentions that he's going into his bedroom to masturbate. This is the crew of people around which you formulate your decisions. There is a saying that we are the people we hang out with. OOOOOFFFF!!!

So maybe you need rent money or you want a really good story for a few years later and you discover that there are men who will pay for you to masturbate in front of them. The standard rate is 150 dollars per private meeting. You decide that 150 bucks is a lot of grocery money or enough money for half a bottle of Winstrol V. You need to take somebody with you to make the whole thing less gay. You find out that Hot Chocolate is into this kind of stuff. You make arrangements to meet him. You both get high beforehand because you want to bond (like jacking off in front of two men isn't going to be enough of a bonding experience). So you smoke a joint with him, not because he's black, but rather he likes joints, regardless of his racial background. You arrive at the man's house. The man happens to be a gay man. Otherwise, it may be weirder. DO NOT SHOW UP AT A STRAIGHT MAN'S HOUSE TO JACK OFF!!!

Make sure that you have the proper address. You will go into a room. The gay man will put on some straight porn. Clearly, he feels like throwing up when he sees it. You must now practice what Stanislavski called the circle of concentration. You must concentrate only on the porn to become aroused and eliminate the thoughts that are arising from the opposite spectrum, which is that you are masturbating in front of two men. Included in those two men are a fat Austrian guy and an incredibly hung "modern savage". Stanislavksi coined the term "circle of concentration" for actors who needed to focus either on their scene partners or on the task at hand to fully immerse themselves in a scene instead of letting inner monologue be dictated by the thought or the preconceived notion of thoughts coming from the audience.

So here you are masturbating in front of two men for money. But then the thought passes through your head, "What if we don't get the money?" Then this would be gay. But the fact that money is involved makes it a bi-curious, hetero-capitalist experience. Stay focused on the porno but simultaneously turn your attention somewhat to the gay man. After all, he is paying to see you masturbate. He is not just paying to see a silhouette of your hip bobbing in the breeze. SHOW THAT FAGGOT SOME COCK! PUMP AWAY LIKE YOU WANT TO EARN 150 BUCKS, YOU HALF-QUEER!

Try to not look at Hot Chocolate's dick. It will scare you. It looks like a python eating a plus-sized beefsteak tomato. Eventually, after much awkwardness, you will be ready to come. Either come all over the towels on the floor or in your hand and throw the come at the gay man. He will love this. He may try to catch it in his mouth; if he does this, he will look like a dolphin jumping for a fish at Sea World. If he catches your come in his mouth, he will get some kind of tonsillitis and you will be gay for a day by consequence. He will probably be too busy huffing poppers to realize you even came. He will be thinking about all the times he was locked in lockers and called fag in high school.

When Hot Chocolate has come and the gay man has come, you will be free to go wash up and collect your 150 dollars. This day will haunt you for the rest of your life. You will see Hot Chocolate the next day and he may steal your money when you're not looking. It's not because he's black, it's because he is a person who likes to steal. Eventually, you will go to therapy. You will never mention this story to anyone, and you will eventually discover that it may work as stand-up comedy. You will tell this story all over the world. The telling of the story has cleansed your soul.

But remember, I told it first.

Proper etiquette for being a middle-aged white man and working your way out of the ghetto

Many of us who can read were not raised under poverty-stricken, community-housing standards in a third-world country like the United States of America. Yes, there is an American dream, but that dream is now financed by China and that dream is no longer what it used to be. That dream can no longer be bought with hard work and perseverance, it must be leased at high interest rates and it must be mortgaged through banks that have been bailed out. That dream is no longer a wife and two and a half kids and a picket fence. The dream may now be a same-sex partner, one adopted child of non-descript color, and a bus pass. The dream is not what it used to be, especially if you have a dream.

As children nurtured outside of the government assistance program, we were taught in the middle and upper classes that we could be whatever we wanted to be. We were taught that dedication and passion would help us accomplish our dreams of fame and fortune. Our upper-middle class parents were wrong. They helped us. They bought us whatever we needed to fit in. They tapered our jeans and got us Converse and bicycles and helped us find summer jobs so that we could afford economy cars in which to finger bang our early conquests. They did not prepare us for the post 9/11/reality television fallout that crushed our beings.

So we found ourselves in our late 20s and early 30s doing what we thought would bring us happiness. We were entrepreneurs. We were making enough to get by; we had significant others, and we thought that we were content. Then we woke up and realized that we were merely a shadow of what our destiny was supposed to be. So we gave it all up and cashed in our chips and moved to a bigger city where dreams could be made. However, when you live in a city where townhomes go for 20 million dollars in the right neighborhood and rents skyrocket quicker than an MTV talking head show about online dating, you realize that you have to start from the bottom.

So you ended up moving to a neighborhood that you hoped was going to gentrify. The gentrified areas were already full of young couples with children and rescued pit-bulls named Cody. You couldn't afford to be gentrified when you were eating failed dreams and ramen noodles for dinner. So you moved to the "yet to be up and coming" neighborhoods. Public transit was still readily accessible, but you were thrown into a world of gangs, drugs, uneducated children and lesser educated parents . . . the American ghetto.

Ghettos have existed in all cultures. Jews still remember the ghettos of Warsaw all the way to the Lower East Side tenement buildings that they occupied as they arrived in droves at Ellis Island in an attempt to find their sideburns and curly hair a nicer bed to lay on, a better life, and a tender pastrami sandwich. So here you find yourself: older than you once were and living in the ghetto. The sirens and the gunshots are consistent if not constant. You feel oddly safe because you think that any aggressor knows that as a white person, you must be crazy to live here unless you were a trained MMA fighter. So you get by.

But your life isn't about getting by. It's about breaking out. You can't stay in the ghetto forever; you are educated, ambitious, and although you are not young anymore, you can still remember what youth was. So you need to bust out of the government cheese neighborhood. Here's how. Follow your predecessors. Model yourself after the successful. Look at most of the people who have broken out of the ghetto and see that in the cases of African

Americans, they were either artists or athletes. The kids rap about the ghetto to get out of the ghetto. They go on to become film directors, producers, or young ingénues. Some of them go on to become stand-up comics and joke about throwing diapers out of project windows and how big the cockroaches were in their bedrooms (that they shared with nine other kids).

A surprisingly high number of them go on to become NFL players. Others become token players in the NHL. The goal here, since you are not athletically gifted and probably can't sing or write rhymes since these are primarily African American predispositions, is to find something easy enough to do where you can hit a big bankroll in one year, establish credit, and then get a decent apartment somewhere that will make these bodegas a thing of the past. Learn how to act or improvise. Both of these things are readily available to study in any major city. Either one of these skills will eventually put you into a position where you can land a couple of TV commercials with stunning residual checks falling in and will give you the credit you need to get out of the ghetto. You have to have hope.

It helps if you don't fall into the trappings of the ghetto lifestyle. Avoid drinking 40s all day on the stoop. Do not adopt a shelter dog. Fight with all your will power against being mistaken for a light-skinned Latino member of the 145th Street Bloods. Try to not gather too many baby mammas. Keep your neck tattoos to a minimum, as they may harm your chances of getting a good Viagra commercial, which would pay triple scale since it takes you out of the saleable market for at least a year. Stay out of prison. Do not commit any drive-bys, if they can be avoided. Sign an agent. Audition for everything you can. All it takes is one commercial to get you out of the Thug Life.

Hopefully, one day soon, you will be dating white girls who go to yoga and you may actually be able to walk home from a bar at night instead of taking a 40-dollar cab. Failing your ability to act, you may want to try voice-over work or stand-up comedy. These may take longer to succeed at, but there is still the off chance of an economic windfall. If none of these brilliant ideas work, write an instructional, quirky book about how all of these aforementioned suggestions failed. And always remember, people with no education got out of the ghetto; if you can't do it, blame it on the education system and go into politics running as the only white candidate in your neighborhood.

About The Author

Originally from Toronto, after graduating with an honors degree in Philosophy from the University of New Brunswick, Aaron began his career as a stand-up comedian at the famous Canadian comedy institution, Yuk Yuk's. After years of crafting an act he began touring Canada and became a headlining comic. Nominated for two Canadian Comedy Awards and winner of the 2007 College Comedian of the year award, it was then time to go international. He has headlined the U.K., the United States, Japan, and Israel as part of the CBC Documentary "A UNIVERSAL LANGUAGE" which follows six comedians on a controversial tour of Israel. Aaron has appeared as part of the Boston Comedy Festival, The New York Comedy Festival, as well as the nationally televised Winnipeg Comedy festival. Aaron also performed his raw brand of stand-up at the world premiere of The Aristocrats film and on the world famous SET LIST show at the best comedy club in NYC ...'The Stand'. Aaron can currently be seen as Floyd on the groundbreaking new television series 24 Hour Rental. Aaron's first one-man show about his venture as a willing participant in the sex trade, The Underbelly Diaries completed an Off-Broadway run at Theatre Row in NYC in 2013 where it was met with critical acclaim. The show was described by New York theatre.com as "Shocking, disgusting (in places) and absolutely hilarious." He also performed an Off-Broadway run of Jeremy Levy's new play '21 days'. Aaron has appeared in the feature films Detroit Rock City, The Ladies Man, The Lookout, The Triumph of Dingus McGraw, and Boondock Saints 2:All Saints Day. Recent television guest appearances include Golden Boy (CBS), Elementary (CBS), Murdoch Mysteries (CBC), KING (SHOWCASE), BREAKOUT KINGS (A&E) and many more....

Aaron now resides in Harlem, NYC and is lonely.

AaronBerg.Com